'HOW TO'
BOOK OF
HOME
DECORATING

HAROLD & ELIZABETH KING

BLANDFORD PRESS
POOLE, DORSET

The **'HOW TO'** Book of Home Decorating explains in straightforward terms, through the use of concise texts, charts, photographs and diagrams, the methods and techniques that will make your decorating and home maintenance a simpler, more successful and rewarding activity.

'HOW TO'

Contents

The 'How To' Book of Home Decorating
was conceived, edited and designed by
Simon Jennings and Company Limited,
42 Maiden Lane, London WC2, England

General Editor: Michael Bowers

Art Direction: Simon Jennings

Text: Harold and Elizabeth King

Illustrations: Arthur Baker, Brian Craiker

Special Photography: John Couzins

Design & Research Assistant: Caroline Peacocke

First published in the United Kingdom 1981
Copyright © 1981 Blandford Press Limited
Link House, West Street, Poole,
Dorset BH15 1LL, England

Text and Illustrations Copyright
© 1981 Simon Jennings and Company Limited

ISBN 07137 1050 0
Printed in Singapore

THE AUTHORS

Harold and Elizabeth
King have written some
16 books in the home-
improvements field.
Harold King has,
additionally, edited
major consumer journals
in this area – some ten
years ago he put his
knowledge into practice
when he built his own
house.
Also a writer on
computer technology,
video and audio
subjects, Harold with
Elizabeth, runs an active
public-relations
consultancy. A simple
approach to the many
problems of home
decorating and
improvements is one of
the hallmarks of his
writing and is one of the
chief characteristics of
the 'How To' Book of
Home Decorating.

Introduction

The necessity to decorate all, or part, of the home, affects all of us at some stage of our lives. For many people the prospect engenders nothing but enthusiasm; for others, perhaps the majority, it is a time of frustration and despair. This book has been written with those people in mind. It is designed to take the pain out of decorating and to provide a choice of approaches that should suit most readers.

Our chief aim has been to present everything in an essentially practical sequence – so that, whether you are going to decorate one room or the whole house, you can tackle the organisation and the work without stress and wasted effort.

Nothing in this book requires the services of a professional decorator or builder. Even the most complicated of the jobs described can be tackled by someone who is attempting it for the first time. We do not deal with structural improvements or alterations, neither do we talk about plumbing or electrical work. On the other hand, you will find a full range of possibilities for walls, ceilings, windows, doors, floors and stairwells etc. – together with the techniques and methods for achieving them. Numerous hints and tips, explained with the help of drawings and diagrams, provide solutions to those many problems which lurk about the house waiting for someone to resolve them. Overall, the aim is to ensure that every job can be undertaken with a sense of proportion and a reasonable certainty that it will not get out of hand.

We do not recommend ways of cutting corners, but we do suggest ways of organizing the work which will result in considerable saving of time and effort. In other words, this is the basic handbook for those people for whom home decorating might otherwise be an unbearable chore.

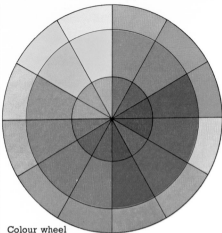

Colour wheel
A colour wheel is a useful aid in planning a harmonious colour scheme. From yellow, at the top, the spectrum proceeds clockwise and colourwise, through the 'cool' colours on the right to the 'warm' colours on the left. The warmth created by a yellow/orange scheme is clearly seen below.

The use of colour

One of the most important ways of establishing your own style in the home is effective use of colour. Used imaginatively, colour can create vista, reduce height, camouflage ill-proportioned rooms, add warmth or coolness – and change or improve the general impression in a variety of other ways.

Colour planning can only be seen as a guideline on which you base your own ideas and achieve individual effects. Never be afraid to experiment.

White, natural light, is made up of all colours of the spectrum, more commonly known as the rainbow colours – red, orange, yellow, green, blue, indigo and violet. Primary colours – red, yellow and blue – cannot be produced by mixing other colours together, but you can achieve over 2,000 distinct colours, using the primaries in varying proportions. Shades are produced by adding black and tints by adding white, to the base colour.

White, grey and black are known as non-colours – but are very important in colour scheming. White reflects light and gives a feeling of spaciousness, while black absorbs it and grey can be used to give a muted effect.

COLOUR AND TINTS | RELATED COLOURS | OPPOSITE COLOURS | WARM AND COOL

A number of colourway schemes can be tried. One is to use one colour with tints and shades of the same colour. The addition of white or grey for contrast will help to prevent dullness.

You may select two related colours – such as blue/purple and purple, red/orange, or two shades of yellow – colours are used in unequal proportions – it may be necessary to make a contrast with areas of white, black or grey.

Equally, you may choose opposite colours – such as those shown here – but they must be used in unequal amounts, or they will certainly clash. Quite interesting colour schemes can be devised by selecting three colours, set at equal distances apart, on the colour wheel.

You can also divide the colour wheel into its warm and cool sides, pairing colours from each side. Here, red-orange and red-purple are shown with yellow-green and blue-green, their cool opposites.

7

How & where to start?

It has been said, that to 'fail to plan is to plan to fail', and nowhere is this more true than in decorating your home.

The general rule, whether working inside or outside, is to start at the top and work downwards. Both inside and outside work require good access equipment. Not only is it easier to use the right equipment for the job, but it is also safer. (see *Safety*).

Exterior

Much depends on the amount of work to be done, but assuming a complete re-decoration job, including wall surfaces, start at the top. Check gutters and downpipes. The plastic type are not usually painted but may be so if you want to do it. Cast-iron guttering needs attention to any rust spots, rubbing down treatment and painting.

Prepare and paint bargeboard and soffits and prepare window joinery. It is not wise to leave unprepared wood or metal for even a minimum of time, so if you have to strip back to the bare material, make sure this is primed with a suitable primer as quickly as possible.

Next tackle the wall surfaces. These may consist of facing brick or be clad in tile, timber, aluminium or plastic. They may be smooth-faced cement blocks, natural or reconstituted stone or rendered in a smooth or textured decorative finish.

Re-rendering or applying a textured finish should be done at this stage. Take care to mask windows and rainwater goods (gutters and downpipes) and to cover paths and driveways as splashes may be difficult to remove later.

Finally, deal with window surrounds, frames, and doors. As you work, make sure that previously decorated surfaces are covered.

Interior decorating

Tackling interior decorating jobs also needs careful planning, especially because so many jobs inside the home will disrupt its normal smooth running.

It makes the job easier if you can clear as much of the area as possible.

Where there are bulky items that cannot be easily removed, move them to the centre of the room and cover with dust sheets.

If possible, remove carpeting. In the case of fitted carpet, cover with polythene sheet stapled down at the edges. Do not use newspaper because this tends to move, leaving areas exposed. It can also be a slippery safety hazard. Preparation of surfaces comes first. Start at the top and work downwards, although floor repairs should be tackled first, especially if this involves such things as sanding wood floors – which creates dust and dirt.

Ceilings may be either papered, painted or distempered. Strip and prepare as necessary. (See *Ceilings*).

Next tackle wall surfaces (see *Walls preparation*) and prepare wood areas, skirtings, architraves, picture rails, windows and doors. (See *Preparation of Woodwork*).

Start general redecoration at the top, i.e. the ceiling. Next prime, or paint as necessary, wood surfaces, window and door-joinery.

If walls are to be papered or given a textured wallcovering this should be applied last of all.

ORGANIZING THE WORK

BUDGETING

Before embarking on any decorating project, consider your expenditure. The budget is an essential part of your planning. Many a good scheme has failed because funds were exhausted halfway through the project.

MAKE THE MOST OF WHAT YOU'VE GOT

Take a very close look at your home before committing yourself to a plan. There may be some interesting features – a hearth, a tiled floor, a window or an alcove that could become the main feature, or the starting point of the design scheme.

MATCHING COLOURS AND MATERIALS

Carpets, curtains and soft furnishings are expensive items, so think about them within the context of the whole scheme – they cannot easily be discarded.

SEQUENCE OF WORK

Keep to the following sequence as a general rule: clear the room, start at the top and work downwards. Be very thorough with your preparation, starting with ceilings, then walls, woodwork and floors.

Decorating walls

Walls can be a vitally important area of home decoration. If they are too high you can achieve a lowering effect by bringing the ceiling colour further down the walls. Walls that are squat will look higher if you remove picture rails and apply paint or paper to the ceiling, cutting out frieze areas. Rooms on the shady side of the house can be made sunny and bright by using the appropriate colours and materials. By utilizing existing features, such as fireplaces (see page 12), alcoves and recesses you can give your rooms new dimensions for a minimum outlay.

Ways with walls

Problem surfaces, such as in kitchens and bathrooms are ideally suited to tiles, *top left*. They are easy to clean and can be matched with other surfaces. The gloss paint in this bathroom, *right*, is simple but luxurious; the plastic panelling, *below left*, is deceptively resistant. Mirror walls, *far left*, may not be everyone's taste, but they create a very light and airy effect. Conventional coordinated colours and materials, *below right*, need not be dull – while hessian, *far right*, is just one of many available textured wallcoverings.

EXISTING FEATURES

Make the most of existing features such as alcoves and recesses; try making a focal point of prominent structures like chimney breasts.

Chimney breasts

In many homes at least one of the living rooms will have a chimney breast. Although they can be removed, it is a messy, structural job which may need building consent. Often they can be utilized to provide a focal-point.

This may be achieved by using a wallcovering on the chimney breast which contrasts with adjoining wall areas, tiling with ceramic or cork tiles, cladding with timber, or panelling. Stone cladding is another possibility, where the material is appropriate, and can be achieved with thin stone 'slipper' bricks.

It may be possible to remove the traditional fireplace surround, enlarge the fireplace opening and inset a larger grate, a decorative stove, even a gas or electric fire. Sometimes it is possible to raise the hearth, which produces a striking effect in the room. Stoves and gas fires must be safely installed on fire-retardent bases and have ducted ventilation.

Popular wall finishes

Wallcoverings

This term covers a wide range of materials, from conventional wallpapers to fabrics and exotic silks. Washable vinyl papers are popular for areas of the home which are particularly subject to condensation, and are easily cleaned. (See the following page and page 66 for further details of wall coverings.)

Paint

Paint, oil-based or water-based emulsion, can be applied on sound, clean wall surfaces. Emulsion paint is used on newly plastered surfaces since this is a porous product, and will allow the plaster to dry out. Oil-based paints should not be used on newly plastered walls. Paint is probably the most versatile wall finish, being available in every colour imaginable and with high gloss, semi-gloss, silk or matt finishes.

Textured wall finishes

These include some of the fabric wallcoverings and also applied textured finishes, such as cement-based textured paint. These materials not only give a textured finish, but they also cover imperfections.

Cork

Cork, in sheet or tile form, is a popular choice for wall finishes. It is available in a range of attractive natural colourways, and even print designs. A cork wall has the advantage of providing a permanent finish with insulant properties. Sheet cork is usually applied in much the same way as other sheet wall coverings, using the adhesive recommended by the manufacturer. Cork tiles, which may be untreated or prefinished with a polyurethane seal, are easily cut, and fixed with a proprietary adhesive.

Timbered Walls

Natural wood, in either pine or plank form, gives an attractive low-maintenance surface. All the natural colours and variations in timber make wood a good choice for wall cladding in almost any area of the home. Wood cladding is available in two main forms: as standard-sized natural or prefinished panels, or solid timber planking – square-edged or tongued-and-grooved. Although both types of cladding are easy to fix, timber panelling is usually quicker.

See pages 16–17 for estimating quantities★

WALL TILES

Ceramic tiles

Glazed, ceramic tiles are available in a wide range of colours and designs, and you can choose from home-made products or imported tiles from countries such as Italy, Portugal and Spain, all with a tradition in producing colour tiles with superb designs. Whether your choice is for plain colours, patterns or sculptured textured finishes, there are ceramic tiles available to fit the profile.

● Mirror Tiles also add interest, and can provide an illusion of space in a small room. Stainless-steel tiles are widely available and give a bright, wipedown surface.

Brick slippers

A number of firms manufacture brick slippers which can be fixed to the surface of the wall to give a natural brick finish.

Stone and slate finishes

Natural stone and slate are two of the materials that are available in wall cladding form and provide attractive wall finishes, requiring no maintenance.

Walls-choice of finish

Choice of texture is as important as colour when deciding on a cool or warm effect for a room. Usually, materials such as cork, timber and hessian will give a warm feeling and mirrors, ceramic tiles and gloss paints will create the opposite effect. Shown here are: **1** Anaglypta/embossed papers; **2** Rough cast plaster; **3** Wood and cork; **4** Ceramics/marble/glass; **5** Foil papers; **6** Vinyls; **7** Textured papers; **8** Printed papers; **9** Hessians; **10** Fabrics; **11** Silks; **12** Paints.

Making a sample board
Before committing yourself to any expenditure, make a sample board of the materials, colours and designs you intend to use. Glue them to a piece of cardboard in roughly the same proportions as you intend to use in your final scheme.

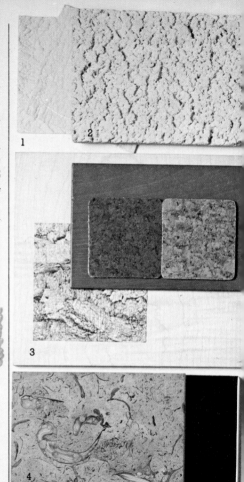

7   8   9   10   11   12

Walls- estimating quantities

Always make sure that you order sufficient materials to complete a particular job. Apart from the inconvenience of running out of materials and finding the shops are shut, you may not always be able to match colours and shades exactly at a later date.

While manufacturers try to ensure a complete match, sometimes – particularly with wallcoverings – colours may vary slightly from batch to batch, or, if you leave the job for a long period, you could find you are trying to match a discontinued design.

Paint guidance as to coverage on given surfaces can only be an approximate indication because the make of paint selected, the method of application and the absorbancy of the surface, will determine how much paint you will actually require.

ESTIMATING PAINT QUANTITIES

This chart gives the approximate quantity of paint required to cover a prepared, non porous surface. Check paint can label or manufacturer's specification before purchasing.

PRIMER COAT			
PINTS	LITRES	SQ YARDS	SQ METRES
9	5	72	60
4.4	2.5	36	30
1.75	1	14.4	12
0.9	500 ml	7	6
0.4	250 ml	3.5	3

TOP COAT			
PINTS	LITRES	SQ YARDS	SQ METRES
9	5	90	75
4.4	2.5	45	37
1.75	1	18	15
0.9	500 ml	9	7.5
0.4	250 ml	4	3.5

EMULSION			
PINTS	LITRES	SQ YARDS	SQ METRES
9	5	108	90
4.4	2.5	54	45
1.75	1	21.6	18
0.9	500 ml	11	9
0.4	250 ml	5.4	4.5

ESTIMATING WALLCOVERING QUANTITIES

A roll of wallpaper is 10 m × 530 mm (11 yds × 21 in) wide. Some European papers are narrower and special papers may come in non-standard sizes. A standard roll of wallcovering covers an area of 5 sq m (6 sq yds.) on a flat surface. Allow a little extra for pattern-matching and cutting-in.

Individual manufacturers can supply details of requirements for pattern-matching of particular products. (See chart).

▼ HEIGHT FROM SKIRTING		DISTANCE AROUND ROOM IN YARDS OR METRES INCLUDING DOORS AND WINDOWS ▼												
mm	ft/in	10	11	12	13	14	15	16	17	18	19	20	21	22
2000–2200	6′6″–7′2″	5	5	5	6	6	7	7	7	8	8	9	9	10
2200–2400	7′2″–7′10″	5	5	6	6	7	7	8	8	9	9	10	10	10
2400–2600	7′10″–8′6″	5	6	6	7	7	8	8	9	9	10	10	11	11
2600–2800	8′6″–9′2″	6	6	7	7	8	8	9	9	10	11	11	12	12
2800–3000	9′2″–9′10″	6	7	7	8	8	9	9	10	11	11	12	12	13
3000–3200	9′10″–10′6″	6	7	8	8	9	10	10	11	11	12	13	13	14
3200–3400	10′6″–11′2″	7	7	8	9	9	10	11	11	12	13	13	14	15
		◄——————————NUMBER OF ROLLS REQUIRED——————————►												

Calculating for Wall tiles

Tiles are produced in standard sizes, 108mm square × 4 mm thick (4¼in × $\frac{3}{16}$in) and 150mm square × 6mm (6in × ¼in) 100mm sq. × 4mm (4in × $\frac{3}{16}$in), and 120mm sq. × 6mm (4¾in × ¼in)

When calculating the number of tiles required allow five per cent extra for cutting and breakages.

If you decide to use 108mm (4¼in) tiles allow three tiles to every 330mm (13in) run, and 72 tiles for every 900mm sq. (36in). Allow for two cut tiles in each row. When using 150mm (6in) tiles allow six full tiles to the running metre, and 36 tiles to a 900mm sq. (36in) area. With border tiles, allow three for every 330mm (13in) run for 108mm (4¼in) tiles and two for every 300mm (12in) run with 150mm (6in) tiles. For window reveal sills, allow one extra spacer tile for each border tile.

Decorating floors

Floors – variety of effects

Floors are often neglected areas in the home. They have to be both hard-wearing, attractive, easy to clean, safe, warm underfoot and capable of taking the day-to-day traffic of feet and the weight of furniture – quite a tough order for any material. The choice of flooring surface is frequently an after-thought, but careful choice of material will enhance a scheme and give a surface that will wear well. Most forms of flooring material are relatively expensive and will not be replaced frequently, so it is important that you select not only the colour and design that pleases you but also the right material for the job.

Additionally, as in all areas in the home, the flooring should be part of the overall effect in colour and texture.

Variety of effects
Today, there are more possibilities for floor coverings than ever before. Traditional pile carpet, *below left*, could be replaced with carpet tiles, *far right*, which have the advantages of being replaceable. It is also possible to arrange your own designs. Vinyl tiles, *right*, and ceramic and quarry tiles, are elegant and easy to maintain. Natural stone, *below*, is perhaps best in a very warm atmosphere. Other natural materials, such as wood, far left, and cork are excellent for creating the farmhouse or cottage effect.

19

Floors-practical considerations

It is important to choose the correct type of flooring for different areas of the home. Most materials discussed in this book can be used in any room, but some are better suited to particular areas and degrees of use and this should be a consideration when choosing flooring materials.

Flooring for kitchens and bathrooms

The criteria for choosing flooring for these rooms is that it should be easily cleaned, non-slip and, particularly in bathrooms, warm and soft underfoot.

Kitchens

There are several possibilities to consider when choosing flooring for kitchens. While some manufacturers do produce a range of kitchen carpeting, the overwhelming choice is for an easy-washed, hygienic flooring surface. Ceramic tiles, quarry tiles, vinyls, in tile or sheet form, cork tiles, or linoleum are all suitable. If you choose ceramic tiles they should be slip-resistant.

Bathrooms

Carpets used in bathrooms should be resistant to damp and be a nylon-based or cotton product. Carpet tiles, which can be moved around to equalise wear, are also a good choice.

Ceramic tiles, again slip-resistant, make for an easy-clean surface, but may need to be laid on a specially braced floor if the tiles are heavy and the area is large. Remember also that they should be laid using waterproof adhesive.

Cork in sheet or tile form, makes an easy-clean, warm to the feet, natural-looking surface. This is available in a range of natural colours, either pre-finished or natural. There are also ranges of attractively printed cork tiles and sheet cork.

Cushion vinyls, in sheet and vinyl tile form are hardwearing surfaces suitable for use in bathrooms.

Other areas of the home

The choice of flooring is really up to you. Many prefer carpeting in the main living areas and in bedrooms. The range both in price and type is enormous. Always take advice when buying carpet. It is expensive and it pays to choose the right carpet for the right area.

Select the quality appropriate to the wear it will receive. For example, it is a waste of money to put a top-quality carpet in a bedroom, where the traffic will be much lighter than in a main living area.

Popular floor finishes

Cork flooring

This is an easy material to lay and gives a warm natural colour to flooring surfaces, It is quite suitable for almost any room in the home and looks attractive in living areas and hallways. It is hard-wearing, easy to care for and has good insulant properties. Maintenance is easy, and cork has the advantage of being non-slip and safe for old people or young children. It is also good for bathrooms and kitchens where a non-slip floor surface is essential.

Vinyl

In both sheet and tile form, this is a hardwearing and attractive flooring surface, offering a wide range of colours, patterns and designs. There are vinyls which simulate wood, marble and other textures.

Although we tend to use them principally in kitchen and bathroom areas, vinyls possess qualities of both durability and design that make them a good choice for hallways, entrances, and living areas.

Wood flooring

Possibly the easiest and cheapest way to achieve a wood floor is to sand and finish existing floorboards. This is quite straightforward provided that the boards are in good condition and of even width (see floor preparation).

Parquet, end-block and woodstrip floor surfacings are not so popular as they used to be because many people find them too difficult to maintain.

This need not be so, because it is possible to buy wood flooring pre-sealed or to apply a hardwearing, poly-urethane finish. If properly finished, wood flooring only needs mopping or a wipe over with a cloth occasionally.

Quarry

From the French *carré* meaning square, these tiles provide a hardwearing flooring surface. They are available in a number of shapes such as hexagonal, octagonal, and incorporate a range of natural colours

Slate and stone

These are hard flooring surfaces suitable for use in kitchens, hallways and living areas.

Floors– choice of finish

Flooring can be very simply divided into two categories: hard and soft finishes. Beyond that, the possibilities are extensive – with new materials, and new versions of old materials, coming on to the market all the time. Remember that, as with wall coverings, texture and finish are as important as colour.

Hard flooring includes wood (strip and block), soft or hardwood boarding, decorative screeds, slate, ceramic tiles, natural stone and quarry tiles.

Soft flooring includes the resilient vinyls – cushion backed or felt backed – vinyl tiles, rubber tiles, linoleum, cork tiles, carpet tiles and carpets.

Flooring finishes ▶
Shown here is a cross-section of flooring materials with a few variations on each.

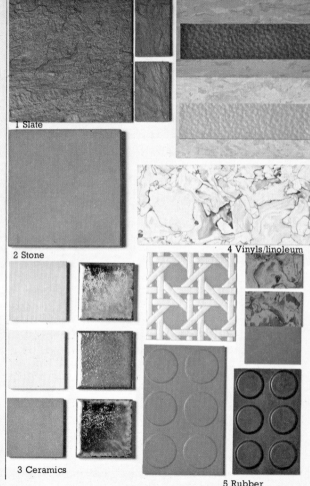

1 Slate

2 Stone

3 Ceramics

4 Vinyls/linoleum

5 Rubber

8 Wood strip

6 Terrazzo

9 Wood block

7 Marble

10 Cork

11 Carpet finishes

23

Floors-estimating quantities

Carpets

Widths of traditional types of carpet are usually from 685mm (27in) up to 2m (79in), although some are now available in a 4m (13ft) broadloom width. They need seaming together carefully.

Estimating for carpeting is really a job best left to the experts, particularly if the carpet is expensive. Equally, fitting, unless you are very skilled, or the carpet is an inexpensive foam-backed one, is also a specialised job.

Carpet tiles

Find the area of the room by multiplying the length by the width. Carpet tiles are made in varying sizes, so you will need to divide the area of the room, by the size of the tile chosen, to find out how many you will need. There may be some wastage to allow for cutting in at room edges and around projections, such as chimney breast areas.

Tiles

Estimating for floor tiles in ceramic, quarry, or for other materials, such as cork, vinyl, or lino is most easily done by drawing a scale plan of the floor area on graph paper. With each square representing one tile, add the number of squares and part squares to calculate the number you will need. To the total amount, add five per cent for cutting in. A patterned tiled floor should also be planned, on graph paper, in the same way. If you want a particular motif or design, count the number of squares needed for this and deduct from the total number required for the area.

Stone and slate

These products are sold by the square metre. Measure the area of the floor, allowing about 5 per cent for wastage in cutting.

◄Carpets
Estimating for carpets is a difficult job and requires familiarity with the material and the methods of fitting it. For carpet tiles, just divide the area of the room by the area of the tile.

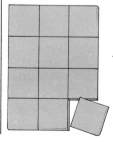

◄Tiles
Draw a plan of the area to be tiled, allowing one square to each tile. You have, then, only to count the tiles. Use this method for designs and motifs.

Sheet flooring

For patterned sheet materials add the depth of one repeat to each length of floor covering.

Sheet flooring is usually sold in 1.22m (4ft), 1.52m (5ft), and 1.83m (6ft) widths but, increasingly, 3m (10ft) to 5m (11ft 6in) widths are available in some ranges of cushion-backed vinyl sheet flooring.

Timber flooring

Find the area of the room and divide this figure by the size of the strip, panel or wood block you intend to use. Manufacturers' literature will usually indicate the expected coverage of the product.

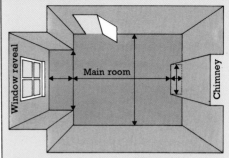

CALCULATING FLOOR AREAS

Window reveal

Main room

Chimney

Calculating the area of floor in a room can sometimes be complicated by projections such as chimney breasts, or recesses. All you have to do is calculate the area of the projection or recess (remembering to use the same units of measurement as for the rest of the room) and subtract from, or add this figure to, the total length × breadth measurement.

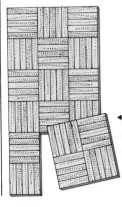

◄ **Block/strip flooring**
Just as for tiles, find the area of the floor and divide by the area of the blocks or strips. Use a calculator when working in inches or millimetres.

◄ **Scaled sketches**
Draw sketch plans on graph paper, choosing a scale to suit the job, e.g. one square to represent one square metre (sq. yd) or one tile etc.

Window treatments

Windows, being the natural light source of every room, deserve careful thought. When you are planning the decorative scheme for the room, think about the natural light and decide how you will handle it in conjunction with the paintwork, wallcoverings, colour scheme and the general atmosphere of the room. The choice of curtains, blinds or shutters will considerably affect the lighting of the interior and will not necessarily improve it although they may enhance the window frame. On the other hand, it is often possible to make vast improvements in the natural light with very simple changes. Some forms of slatted blinds, for example, can give the impression of a warm external light source where, in fact, very little exists. Others, such as Venetian blinds, will diffuse the glare of harsh sunlight into a soft, comfortable light. Coordinated wallcoverings and curtains can be used to make a room lighter or darker, and shutters can be used in conjunction with curtains or blinds. It is all a matter of choice, but a choice which will affect the entire room and will make or mar your decorative scheme.

Decorating with light
Slatted or Venetian
blinds, *right*, can be
used to tone with the
general decor, and to
make the light warmer
or cooler. The dark
colours of the
coordinated scheme,
below right, actually
emphasise the strength
of the light source,
while the Roman blind,
below left, diffuses
strong light with a
warm glow. If your
choice is for curtains,
consider a curtain
track running all
round the room, *top
left*, and use them
alternatively as wall
drapes. Stained glass,
below, can be a very
attractive feature,
where there is a
strong light source.

WINDOW GLAZING

Glazing

Windows may be single or double-glazed, glazed with leaded glass or decorative textured glass.

● There are two types of clear glass available in three grades. **Sheet glass** is usually used for domestic glazing and is available in 3mm–6mm ($\frac{1}{8}$–$\frac{1}{4}$in) thicknesses.

● **Float glass,** in thicknesses of 5–25mm ($\frac{3}{16}$in–1in), is both strong and distortion-free. It is more often used for large picture window areas. This glass may be plain or decorative.

● Decorative **textured glass**, often called 'modesty' glass, is used for glazing in bathroom and toilet areas. The degree of transparency depends largely on the pattern used. It is available in 3mm–5mm ($\frac{1}{8}$–$\frac{1}{4}$in) thicknesses.

● **Wire-mesh glass,** accepted as a fire-retardent material, in $\frac{1}{4}$in (6mm) thickness, is available for use in porches and areas where safety is a factor. Toughened glass is suitable for use in areas where there is a risk of impact, such as doors. The glass, if broken, shatters into granules, not sharp splinters.

● **Solar glass**, available as float, laminated or patterned glass, reduces heat transmission, and glare.

Blinds and curtains

Blinds

There are two basic types of window blind – roller and venetian. Roller blinds, in fabric, often with a plasticised finish are available in a wide variety of colours and designs. To achieve a unified scheme look you can use coordinating fabrics for blinds, curtains and wallcoverings.

Venetian blinds, permit privacy yet allow light into the room. They can be tilted to cut glare and are often useful where the view outside the room is less than attractive. Venetian blinds are usually made of plasticised metal for easy cleaning, though wooden slatted blinds are available.

Other types of blinds include vertical *louvre blinds* which tilt to allow filtered light into the room or pull back for maximum light. *Roman blinds* which roll up in soft folds and those made of *Pinoleum* – thin slats of wood. The latter can be rolled up completely or let down to provide shade but they do not give privacy.

Blinds must be firmly fixed to the wall. Most consist of a head rail or pole which slots into side fixing brackets. The brackets usually fit into the window reveal, screw fixed into plugged holes.

Make sure you fix into a firm wall surface and not just plaster. Blinds can be used decoratively in other areas in the home – as bed headboards, decorative wall hangings, as fronts to open shelving or, in the case of vertical louvre blinds, to divide one area of the home from another.

Curtain tracks and poles

There are numerous ways of suspending curtains. Traditionally the most popular method was a curtain rail, often hidden by a box pelmet in wood or hardboard covered with fabric to match the curtains.

Many curtain tracking systems are now available and headed tapes, sewn to the top of the curtains, give a decorative heading which obviates the need for a pelmet. Curtain poles, in wood, metal and plastic are very popular. Poles in timber and metal are meant to be decorative, and the fixing brackets often echo the design of the poles.

Curtain tracking and poles must be securely fixed. In detail the fixings may differ according to the type, but the basic method is to fix them into the wall, below the plaster surface into pre-drilled and plugged holes.

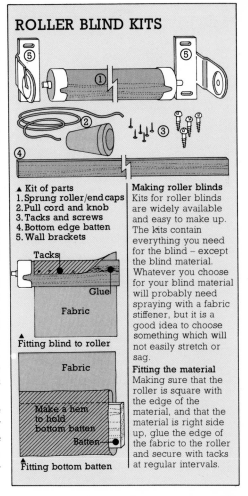

ROLLER BLIND KITS

▲ Kit of parts
1. Sprung roller/end caps
2. Pull cord and knob
3. Tacks and screws
4. Bottom edge batten
5. Wall brackets

Tacks

Glue

Fabric

▲ Fitting blind to roller

Fabric

Make a hem to hold bottom batten

Batten

▲ Fitting bottom batten

Making roller blinds
Kits for roller blinds are widely available and easy to make up. The kits contain everything you need for the blind – except the blind material. Whatever you choose for your blind material will probably need spraying with a fabric stiffener, but it is a good idea to choose something which will not easily stretch or sag.

Fitting the material
Making sure that the roller is square with the edge of the material, and that the material is right side up, glue the edge of the fabric to the roller and secure with tacks at regular intervals.

Decorating ceilings

Often, when planning decorative schemes, the ceiling tends to be a forgotten area – but the range of available finishes is as extensive as for any other part of the house.

Where ceiling areas are blemished, the best solution may be to line, either with a plain lining paper or an embossed or woodchip paper. These give texture and camouflage to minor irregularities in the surface.

Alternatively, tile panels may be applied. These could be acoustic tiles made from fibre board in various finishes, or polystyrene. Polystyrene sheet may also be used. These products not only give a 'new' surface but have insulating properties.

Ceilings may also be timbered. Usually this will be timber panelling or tongued-and-grooved board; both must be fixed to a timber batten framework.

If you wish to reduce the height of a room you could install an illuminated ceiling. They vary in detail, from manufacturer to manufacturer, but usually consist of a plastic or aluminium lattice framework supporting translucent PVC panels. They are available in a range of colours and textures.

Ceiling choice

Ceilings often seem to require some degree of disguise. High ceilings present problems; where the proportions of the room are to be retained, a darker colour on ceiling and frieze, *top left*, may be the answer. Exposing the joists, and suspending attractive objects, *right*, is a simple and effective solution; suspended aluminium panels, *below*, may appeal to science fiction enthusiasts. Low ceilings with exposed beams, *below right*, may benefit from taking the wall colour or covering on to the ceiling. Wood panelling, *bottom left*, is expensive but gives the warmest and most natural effect.

31

Working with ladders

GENERAL SAFETY

Safety, when tackling any decorating job around the home, should be your prime concern. Safety, not only for yourself while you are working, but for others at all times.

The number of jobs which involve some element of risk, particularly where power tools are involved, is almost frightening. However, with care and forethought, home decorating should prove a relatively harmless occupation.

Always buy or hire good-quality access equipment such as ladders, trestles or access towers.

Ladders should never be painted or varnished – this can hide defects. Always check rungs of wooden ladders before using them.

How to carry a ladder
Carry on the shoulder with most of the weight in front.

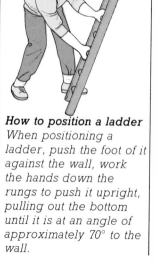

How to position a ladder
When positioning a ladder, push the foot of it against the wall, work the hands down the rungs to push it upright, pulling out the bottom until it is at an angle of approximately 70° to the wall.

SECURING LADDERS

Preventing slide
A sack of sand or soil placed behind the uprights will hold the ladder.

Securing on soft ground
On soft ground, place the base of the ladder on a board to spread the weight, tilting the board to prevent the ladder sliding forward from the vertical surface.

Top fixing
Never lean a ladder against guttering. If you need to top fix, secure a gutter rung to a ladder bracket or tie the ladder to an eye-screw driven into the fascia.

Tying-in ladders
Tie-in the ladder, selecting a convenient projection, or fix to a batten placed behind a section of window frame.

Climbing ladders
When climbing a ladder keep your eyes on the wall in front of you. Do not work from the top rung. Wear shoes that allow you to 'feel' the rungs and make sure any laces are securely tied. Trouser bottoms should be tucked into your socks or secured with cycle clips.

SAFETY TIPS

Leaning too far
Always maintain your centre of gravity in the middle of the ladder. It is tempting to reach just that little bit further, but wiser to re-position the ladder.

Carrying tools
Carry items such as abrasive papers, cloths and brushes in your pockets. Sharp objects – knives, scrapers, paint hooks should be held in the hand. If you do slip they can easily be thrown clear. Large items should be passed up on a line. If you are right-handed work from the right, and vice versa.

Keeping a grip
Keep one hand free to hold the ladder. When painting use an 'S' hook to suspend the paint kettle from a convenient rung.

Working outside

For painting the exterior you will need an extension ladder. Lightweight aluminium ladders are easier to handle but they conduct electricity so keep clear of any overhead electricity supply. Make sure that timber ladders are in perfect condition.

Extension ladders

Suitable for the average two-storey home, they are usually in two sections, one fixed, one sliding. A ladder 4.5m (15ft) long extending to 7.3m (24ft) should be sufficient for most purposes.

Roof work

If you have to work on the roof of your home you should use a well-secured cat-ladder. Walking on roof areas, particularly those consisting of asbestos cement, is both hazardous and likely to cause damage.

Towers

You can buy or hire a sectional tower – sections of tubular scaffolding slotting together to provide platform access.

Towers can be moved easily from area to area and they have lockable castors. Make sure toe boards are fitted to the working platforms; they help to prevent dropped objects from falling to the ground. Scaffold towers should stand on firm, level ground with a

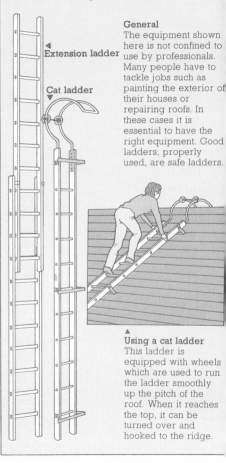

ACCESS EQUIPMENT

◄ Extension ladder

Cat ladder ▼

General

The equipment shown here is not confined to use by professionals. Many people have to tackle jobs such as painting the exterior of their houses or repairing roofs. In these cases it is essential to have the right equipment. Good ladders, properly used, are safe ladders.

▲
Using a cat ladder

This ladder is equipped with wheels which are used to run the ladder smoothly up the pitch of the roof. When it reaches the top, it can be turned over and hooked to the ridge.

ladder securely fixed to the side. The construction of towers allows them to be climbed with safety and ease. If you have a large surface area to work across you may need two towers. They can be bridged with special timber staging.

Carefully inspect all hire items before accepting them. Rusty scaffolding and less-than-perfect boards are a danger.

Working inside

It is all too easy to compromise with access equipment in the home. Most homes have a pair of household steps, in timber, steel or aluminium, but they should be inspected regularly for deterioration, damaged ropes and so on.

Never be tempted to stand on a stool or chair especially when decorating. Ladders, combination ladders and trestles, or a system of ladders and scaffold boards, should be used.

Platform steps, which have a platform at the top which folds back to the rear stiles when the ladder is not in use, are very useful for household access.

Using the right access equipment allows you to tackle the job more easily, safely and efficiently.

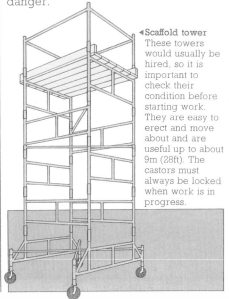

◄**Scaffold tower**
These towers would usually be hired, so it is important to check their condition before starting work. They are easy to erect and move about and are useful up to about 9m (28ft). The castors must always be locked when work is in progress.

Hand rail

Platform for paint and tools

Platform steps►
These are ideal for indoor decorating, especially where it is necessary to have both hands free. The platform is useful for holding tools and paint vessels.

35

Power tool safety

Power tools, especially those designed for preparing surfaces are valuable decorating aids. However, they are dangerous unless used correctly. Always follow the manufacturers' operating instructions.

Electrical safety
If you have to make adjustments to a tool, make sure it is first unplugged. Always use a correctly fused plug and make sure that the cord is in good condition.

Handling
Never pick up a power tool by its cord and keep all electrical equipment out of the reach of children.

Protection
When using tools on abrasive surfaces, wear shatterproof spectacles to protect the eyes, and a mask to protect the lungs.

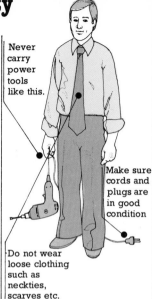

Never carry power tools like this.

Make sure cords and plugs are in good condition

Do not wear loose clothing such as neckties, scarves etc.

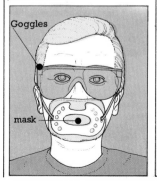

Goggles

mask

PAINT STRIPPING

This involves using a chemical stripper, which may be flammable, or a blow-torch. Use the stripper in a well-ventilated room, do not smoke or use the chemical near naked flames. Always use blow-torches with great care and turn off when not being used. Never use a blow-torch near glass because the heat will crack it. Stripped paint is highly flammable and the waste should never be burnt – neither should sawdust which can 'explode' on ignition.

Handling glass

Glass
Glass should be handled with great care. Never leave pieces of broken glass lying around and, if you cannot immediately reglaze, either tape up the damaged area or tack a piece of card over the window.

Carrying glass▶
Use folded newspaper as 'laps' when carrying glass. Carry vertically and grip gently but firmly. Remember to allow enough room for the glass when negotiating sharp bends.

Carrying large sheets
Large sheets should be carried by two people: the leading person adopting the stance of a single person holding a large sheet, the second supporting the glass with one hand cupped round the lower bottom corner, with the back edge against the shoulder and holding the top edge in the other hand.

Broken glass▶
When removing broken glass wear thick gloves. Glaziers also protect their wrists with bandages.

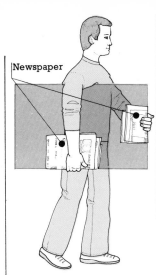

Newspaper

The correct way to carry glass

Removing broken glass

POISONS

Many paint strippers and cleaners may contain toxic or flammable constituents. Ensure that they are used according to manufacturer's instructions. Store properly out of the reach of children and pets. Never put such things as white spirit into other household containers such as lemonade bottles. If you have to remove a product from a manufacturer's container always ensure that the substitute container is clearly marked.

Paint brushes

Brushes, rollers and pads come in many sizes and qualities, most designed to do special decorating jobs. As in all aspects of decorating, it pays to buy the best tools you can afford.

The *filling*, the correct name for the 'business end' of a brush, in the best brushes is of pure bristle. The best bristle comes from China or Russia and can account for up to 90 per cent of the cost of a good brush. Indian bristle is also used, but it is less oily, resilient and hardwearing in use.

Bristle has many advantages, but probably the most important is that its natural taper helps the individual bristles to lay together with a resulting smoother action. The roughened surface of each bristle has little barbs and split tips, known as 'flags' which help to hold the paint.

Synthetic fibre, mixtures of bristle and natural fibre, palm fibre, weasel, horse, squirrel and badger hair are also used as fillings.

A mixture of bristle and a synthetic fibre, such as nylon, will not hold the paint as well as pure bristle and a wholly synthetic fibre will have little paint holding qualities. Buy the best you can afford and maintain them well.

CHOOSING PAINT BRUSHES

When choosing a brush, test the filling by flexing it through the hand – it should feel soft. A good, wide brush, say 75mm (3in) wide, should have bristles 75mm (3in) long and be about 20mm ($\frac{3}{4}$in) thick. Less expensive brushes may be thinner and the filling shorter.

Types of paintbrush

Brushes come in three types – standard, flat and sash. These range in size from 35mm (1$\frac{1}{2}$in) to 100mm (4in) wide, suitable for painting smaller areas, and up to 150mm (6in) and 175mm (7in) wide for larger areas. Large distemper or emulsion brushes are available, but except for professional use, it is not necessary to buy an expensive example.

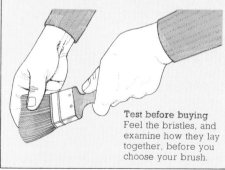

Test before buying
Feel the bristles, and examine how they lay together, before you choose your brush.

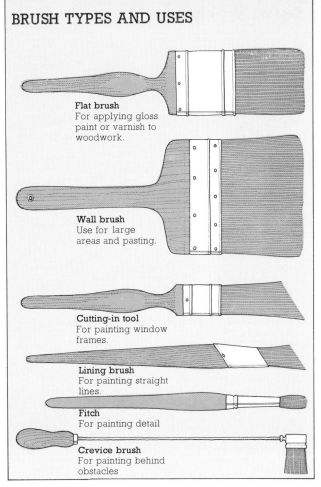

SPECIAL BRUSHES

Cutting-in brush
Used for painting along edges or where fine control of the paint is necessary. The ends of the filling are cut to a bevel.

Crevice or radiator brushes
For painting into awkward corners. These have a flexible metal handle which can be bent to a convenient working angle.

Dusting brushes
Used for dusting down the surface before starting work.

Flat lining brushes
For detailed work such as mouldings.

Fitches
Used for painting mouldings.

Paper-hanging brush
For smoothing out wallpaper when pasting to wall.

BRUSH TYPES AND USES

Flat brush
For applying gloss paint or varnish to woodwork.

Wall brush
Use for large areas and pasting.

Cutting-in tool
For painting window frames.

Lining brush
For painting straight lines.

Fitch
For painting detail

Crevice brush
For painting behind obstacles

Paint brush maintenance

Cleaning

Brushes should always be thoroughly cleaned after use. Use the correct type of solvent for the paint. Emulsion and other water-based paints can be removed with water. Paraffin or white spirit is used to remove oil-based paints and polyurethanes while the paint is still fluid. Use methylated spirit to remove spirit varnish.

Amyl-acetate, mixed with wood naptha, will remove cellulose paint. Rubber-based paint can be removed with petrol. Paintbrushes can be cleaned with one of a number of reliable brands of cleaner.

Once you have removed as much of an oil-based paint as possible, give it a final cleanse in hot, soapy water, then rinse thoroughly and allow to dry. If paint has been allowed to harden in the filling, it may be difficult to remove later. The only possibility then, is to suspend the filling in a proprietary brush cleanser for a few days. Do not allow the brush to rest on the bristles because it will bend and 'cripple' the filling.

Short-term cleaning

If you intend to leave the brush for a short period before resuming work,

remove as much of the paint as possible against the side of the paint container and then suspend the filling in a container of the appropriate solvent.

Drill a hole in the handle of the brush, if one is lacking – some have a hole predrilled for this purpose – and insert a long nail or a piece of stiff wire which will rest across the top of the container.

PAINT SOLVENTS	
Paint type	**Correct solvent**
Emulsion paint Distemper Water based paints	Warm water – with some detergent or washing up liquid
Oil based paints Polyurethanes	White spirit, turpentine substitute or paraffin
Spirit varnish	Methylated spirit
Cellulose paint	Amylacetate and wood naptha
Rubber based paint	Petrol

◄ **Short term cleaning or soaking hard brushes**
Drill a hole in the handle of the brush, insert a long nail or a piece of wire and suspend in the correct solvent.

Brush storage

BRUSH CLEANING

1. Remove surplus paint

2. Brush out the remainder

3. Clean in hot soapy water

Storing brushes

Once you have finished with the brushes, they should be cleaned carefully and stored with care. Check that the filling is completely dry and then wrap in either newspaper or brown-paper. Secure with a rubber band round the head of the brush and store flat. From time to time, check the condition of the brushes. If the filling is of bristle, store with mothballs. Moths have a predeliction for paint-brush filling.

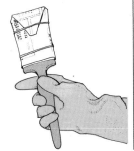

NEW BRUSHES

Using a new brush

'Flirt' the bristles against the palm of your hand before using the brush – this helps to remove dust and any loose bristles.

Do not use a completely new brush on a final decorative surface. Always give it a proving run on an undercoat, because even the most thoroughbred of brushes sheds a few bristles the first time it is used.

Painting equipment

Rollers

Paint rollers are useful for covering large areas such as ceilings and walls, but they do use more paint. Rollers are available in a range of sizes from 25mm (1in) to 250mm (10in) – a good, general-purpose size would be 200mm (8in). Plastic hair, nylon foam or, most expensively, lamb's wool, are generally used for rollers.

Nylon-foam rollers, apart from being less expensive, are easier to clean. They are best used for applying water-based paints, such as emulsion, and for undercoats. Use a lambs' wool roller for top coats because they give a finer finish.

After use, clean the roller, using the correct solvent for the paint. Rinse it thoroughly and allow to dry completely before storing in newspaper or brown-paper.

Paint trays

Paint trays, designed for use with rollers, may be of metal or plastic. Always make sure they are dust free before using. To load, strain the paint into the tray and roll the roller into it.

Paint kettles

Paint kettles, in either plastic or metal, are a necessary aid. They allow you to dispense a usable amount of paint from the main container which can then be closed to prevent a skin forming on the paint. Suspended from an 'S' hook, the kettle can be hung on a ladder or positioned near the work thus leaving both hands free.

Paint pads

Paint pads, in plastic, foam or lamb's wool, can be used as an alternative to paint brushes. They come in a range of sizes and some have replaceable pads. Cleaning and storage methods are similar to those for brushes.

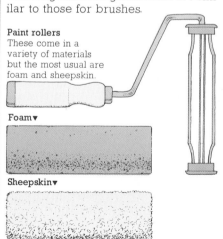

Paint rollers
These come in a variety of materials but the most usual are foam and sheepskin.

Foam▼

Sheepskin▼

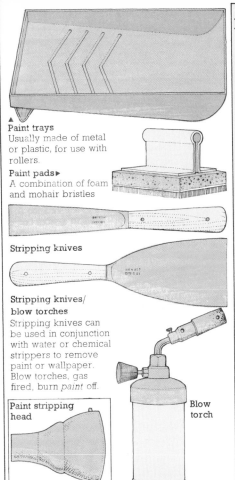

Paint trays
Usually made of metal
or plastic, for use with
rollers.

Paint pads▶
A combination of foam
and mohair bristles

Stripping knives

**Stripping knives/
blow torches**
Stripping knives can
be used in conjunction
with water or chemical
strippers to remove
paint or wallpaper.
Blow torches, gas
fired, burn *paint* off.

**Paint stripping
head**

**Blow
torch**

PAINT STRIPPING EQUIPMENT

Stripping knives and shave-hooks
Two stripping knives and two shave-hooks will be very useful aids. There are two types of shave-hook, one multi-edged, the other triangular. They are used with a blow-torch to remove paint from areas such as mouldings.

Blow-torches
Modern blow-torches are usually gas fired. They can either have a replacement gas canister or be attached by a flex to a larger canister. The flame is adjustable at the head of the torch.

When stripping paint, use the paint stripping head in conjunction with a stripping knife.

Care
Make sure that knives and shave hooks are clean and sharp and that the blow-torch is stored with gas turned off.

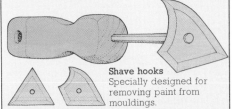

Shave hooks
Specially designed for
removing paint from
mouldings.

43

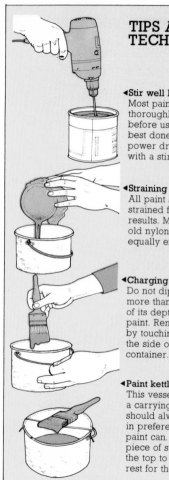

◄**Stir well before use**
Most paints must be
thoroughly stirred
before use. This is
best done with a
power drill equipped
with a stirrer.

◄**Straining**
All paint should be
strained for the best
results. Muslin, or an
old nylon stocking, are
equally effective.

◄**Charging the brush**
Do not dip the brush
more than two thirds
of its depth into the
paint. Remove excess
by touching against
the side of the
container.

◄**Paint kettles**
This vessel, which has
a carrying handle,
should always be used
in preference to the
paint can. Stretch a
piece of string across
the top to provide a
rest for the brush.

Applying paint

When you open a new tin of paint, you
may find a layer of oil or thinners on top;
this must be thoroughly stirred in. On a
previously opened can, you may find
that a skin has formed on top; this must
be removed. Never stir it in, because it
will not mix and the paint will be 'bitty'.

With the exception of thixotropic
paints (gell), all should be thoroughly
stirred before use. You can use a piece
of clean timber or a paint stirrer attachment with a power drill. The paint is at
the right consistency when it flows
evenly from the tip of the stirrer.

Strain all paint before use. An old
nylon stocking makes an excellent
strainer.

Use a paint kettle when painting.
This has two advantages: one, if you
spill the paint, you do not waste too
much, and secondly, you can shut the
lid of the can thus keeping the dust out
and helping to prevent a skin from
forming on the paint surface.

When 'charging' the brush, do not
dip the filling more than two thirds of
the way into the paint. Lightly touch the
filling against the side of the paint.
kettle to remove excess paint. Once the
brush has been charged in this way, it is
not then necessary to dip the filling

more than a third of the way into the paint.

To rest the brush while working, either use a magnetic clip fixed to the side of the kettle or stretch a piece of string taughtly across the kettle and lay the brush across this. (See page 40.)

Using a paint roller

Pour about 1in (25mm) of strained paint into the lower stope of the tray. Dip the roller in the paint and roll it up towards the higher end.

When painting, work slowly and evenly, from the top to the bottom of the work, using a herringbone stroke.

Finally, work vertically downwards, reloading the roller as necessary. If you are using gloss paints, complete a section before working vertically.

Emulsion paint should be thinned with water to about 50 per cent for the first coat. Gell paints must be stirred, until the paint flows evenly, for application with a roller. Never do so when using a brush.

Successful painting requires a certain amount of skill, but it is a skill which is fairly easy to acquire. If you follow the tips and techniques described in these pages it is unlikely that you will go very far wrong.

CHOOSING PAINT

Painting for interior surfaces

Full gloss, semi gloss, eggshell or flat-finish paints are all suitable for interior painting – as are water-based emulsions. Where the area is exposed to intensive sunlight, or in areas subject to condensation, use a hard-wearing gloss.

◄Paint choice
Gloss paints are best for woodwork, exteriors and any surface which has to take a lot of wear. Modern vinyl paints give smooth, even finishes, but are less hard wearing.

Exterior surfaces

Use a hard-gloss paint with the recommended undercoat. On bare softwood, apply a primer coat, an undercoat, then two top coats. This is known as a four-coat system.

◄Four coat system
This system is usually applied to surfaces which have not previous been painted. It may seem tedious, but the results will be worth the effort.

PREPARATION

First fill any cracks, prime and rub down. Once the primer has dried, use a wet abrasive paper to smooth the surface and then wipe clean with a damp cloth. Apply an undercoat. This helps to give a dense base for the top coat. Rub down the surface between each application with a wet abrasive or fine glass paper. When applying two top coats, either apply one eggshell and one gloss, or two gloss coats (the second is a little more difficult to apply).

Undercoating
Undercoat takes between 16 and 20 hours to dry, after which time the surface should be rubbed down gently and cleaned with a tack cloth.

Painting techniques

When painting large areas, divide the work into sections. Brush from left to right, working slightly downwards, then brush up and down. This will give an even spread of paint.

Do not overload the brush when dipping into the paint. Dip the brush about 13mm (5in) into the paint, and touch it against the inside of the paint kettle. Work freehand but, for tricky areas, you may find it easier to use the back of another brush as a rest.

Paint towards the edges and the 'wet' edge. On areas such as doors, use a smaller brush to 'lay off'. Always work in a continuous sequence and do not allow one section to get too dry before you paint the next. If this happens, you will not be able to blend the two areas and the result will be an obvious demarcation.

When using polyurethane paints, which dry quickly, paint may tend to 'drag' on the brush – if this happens, add a little white spirit to the paint. When painting areas such as corners, jab the paint in with the tip of the brush and then brush downwards. Using the technique described as 'laying off' will help prevent unsightly raised edges of paint.

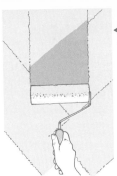

◄Working with a roller
A roller should be worked with overlapping diagonal strokes. Again, begin at the top and work downwards. Follow the diagonal strokes with up and down working.

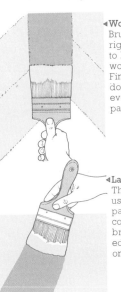

◄Working with a brush
Brush from left to right, then from right to left – all the time working downwards. Finally, brush up and down. This ensures an even coverage of paint.

◄Laying off
This is a technique used at the edge of the painted area. It consists of lifting the brush towards the edge and painting only with the tip.

LAYING OFF AND CUTTING IN

'Laying off'

'Laying off' means that for the final brush strokes, you use the tip of the bristles in an upward lifting motion. Always lay-off in the direction of the wood grain. On metal and other surfaces, lay off in the longest direction. Laying off across the grain will raise the grain and make the paint film uneven.

Always 'lay-off' in one direction only when applying paint. If you alternate directions, the result will be uneven coverage and a patched effect. Lay off at the edge of a surface only; if you attempt to use the technique in the centre of the work, you will leave brush marks.

'Cutting-in'

The technique of 'cutting-in' is used where you need to paint a fine demarcation line. This may be on windows, where the window frame meets the glass, or where one paint colour adjoins another. You can use an angled brush, called a cutting-in tool, or an old clean brush, worn to an angle. For most cutting-in jobs, a 25mm (1in) wide cutting tool or brush should be used.

47

Painting doors

Before starting to paint doors, remove any door furniture such as handles, catches, hooks, bolts and letter-boxes,. If left in place, however carefully you work, they may get splashed. Also, it is much easier to work if all obstructions are removed. A wedge of newspaper positioned under the door will prevent it from moving as you work. Timber and metal doors should be prepared as necessary (see page 52) before painting. Doors are painted in a specific sequence, dependent on the type of door.

Remove door fittings
Painting doors is much easier if the handle, letter-box plate and lock fittings are removed. Be careful not to get paint into the lock mechanism.

PAINTING A FLUSH DOOR

Flush doors
Flush doors present a large area to paint without leaving demarcation lines. Divide the door into three equal horizontal sections. Start work at the top left-hand corner using a 75mm (3in) brush.

Paint a vertical strip about 450mm (17½in) wide, then another parallel with the first. Cross-brush the two strips of paint evenly into each other and 'lay off' the paint vertically.

Repeat this painting sequence in each section. When you have

1. Paint a vertical strip about 450mm (17½in) wide.

2. Paint a second strip parallel with the first.

3. Paint crossing brush strokes, blending the paint evenly.

completed the three, brush lightly upwards to join the sections.

This needs to be done in one operation, particularly if you are using a quick drying paint.

On exterior opening doors, paint both the top and bottom edges to help prevent water soaking into the wood causing it to swell and the paint to peel.

After painting doors, paint the architrave – the frame round the door.

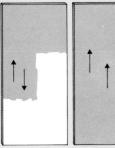

4. Lay off the paint vertically. See page 47 for the appropriate technique.

5. Repeat the sequence from one to four over the rest of the door.

6. Brush lightly upwards to blend the sections of paint together.

PAINTING A PANEL DOOR

Panelled and Cruciform doors
The order for painting a conventional, panelled or cruciform door is: first paint mouldings, then panelled areas and, finally, the stiles (these are the wider sections, dividing the panels). Start work at the top of the door and paint the top, middle, lock and bottom rails, in that order. By working to the sequence shown, you will ensure even paint cover, without visible demarcation lines.

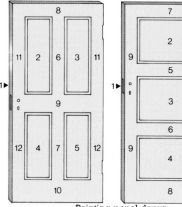

Painting panel doors
Work in the sequence shown, depending on the type of panel door you have

49

Painting window frames

PAINTING A CASEMENT

Casement windows are usually a combination of fixed lights and top opening, or opening side hung vents. The painting order for casement windows is as shown. Never paint too thickly on the closing surfaces of opening windows, this is particularly important on metal frames, as they may stick.

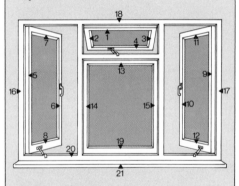

Casement windows
The sequence for painting casement windows, or windows of similar construction, is as shown above. A casement constructed from sash frames would be painted in the same sequence. Avoid getting paint on the cords of sash windows.

Paint helps to provide the waterproof seal between the glass and the window frame, but it is difficult to remove from glass, so use masking tape or a piece of card to protect the glass as you work. Make sure, if you use card, that you keep its edges clean.

When painting metal frames, paint just on to the edge of the glass. This forms a watertight seal, preventing moisture seeping between the putty and the frame and causing corrosion.

If you do get paint on the glass it can be removed with a scraper. It does, however, make sense to remove paint splashes with a damp cloth as you work. When preparing window areas use a chemical paint stripper and a stripping knife. A blowtorch flame may well crack the glass.

Razor blade scraper

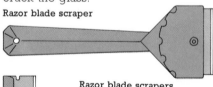

One sided blade

Razor blade scrapers
These consist of specially designed handles which hold ordinary blades and make effective scrapers. One sided blades can be used by holding the clamped metal edge.

Helpful hints

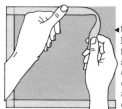

Using masking tape
Masking tape is useful for preventing the spread of paint onto other surfaces, such as glass, and for making a straight line of demarcation.

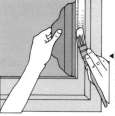

Paint shield
This has the same benefits as masking tape, but it can be used and adjusted with the free hand.

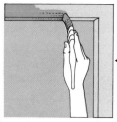

Use the right brush
When painting close to other areas, such as windows, be sure to use the correct brush. See page 43.

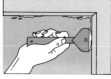

Clean as you go
If paint does get onto the glass, scrape it off before it has time to harden.

PAINTING A SASH WINDOW

Sash windows should be closed before painting starts. Work in the order shown. Do not apply paint thickly to the pulley stile and staff, or the parting beads, because thick paint on these may cause the windows to stick. The sash cord must not be painted because this will stiffen the fibres and may cause them to snap as they pass over the pulleys.

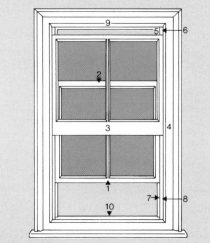

Sash windows
Conventional sash windows should be painted in the sequence shown above.

PREPARING TIMBER

On sound timber work it will only be necessary to wash down with a sugar soap or detergent solution. On large areas, such as doors, start at the bottom and work upwards. This prevents dirt streaks from forming on the door. Wash twice, then rinse finally with clean water, starting at the top on large areas.

'Keying' surfaces
Slight irregularities can be rubbed down with a fine glasspaper, but make sure the surface is dust-free and dry before starting to paint. Rubbing down provides a 'key' for the paint.

Using sanders

To remove old paint use either a hand block sander, a disc or orbital sander or a sanding attachment to a power tool. Wear goggles when using the power tool. (See Safety). Use a power tool with a sanding backing pad and disc. For a fine finish, use an orbital sander. Orbital sanders rotate over the surface and are used for light 'keying' work. Disc sanders, work with a rotary action. Work with the disc at 30° to the timber to minimize swirl marks. Disc-sanders should be used first with coarse paper, working through to fine. Finish sanding with a hand block and a fine paper. You may, of course, prefer to remove the paint with chemical stripper and use the sander to provide the finish.

Disc sander

Orbital sander

SAFETY●

Always wear a face mask and goggles when using power sanders.

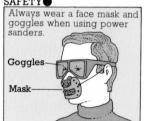

Goggles

Mask

Using chemicals & torches

Strip old paint using either a chemical stripper applied to the surface with a paintbrush, or a gas blow-torch. Avoid getting chemical strippers on the skin. If you do, wash off immediately with cold water. Wash down the surface with white spirit after using a chemical stripper. Use a gas blow-torch, fitted with a paint-stripping head and keep it moving from side to side to avoid charring the timber. Once the paint bubbles, lift it off with a flat stripping knife in an upwards direction. Do not use a blow torch near glass. A certain amount of skill is required to make effective use of a blow torch, so it may be wise to practise on an old piece of painted wood.

Apply stripper with brush

Use stripping head on blow torch

Lift paint with stripping knife

NEW TIMBER

All new timber should be primed and knotted with patent knotting. On porous wood use two coats. On resinous woods you may need to apply an aluminium sealer to prevent resin seepage through the decorative coat. You will not need to do this if you are using varnish, applied coat on coat. The first coat should be diluted by 50 per cent with white spirit.

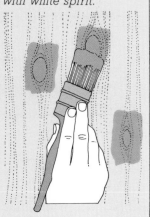

Paintwork-minor repairs

PREPARING METAL

Metal door and window frames must be rubbed down using a wire brush. If you use a wire disc attachment in a power tool, wear shatter-proof goggles. (See Safety). Remove all rust, rub down with emery paper, then apply a rust-neutralising agent before applying a metal primer. On frames needing reglazing, remove the glass and putty before treating the metal. Cellulose paints can be loosened with cellulose thinner. Brush on, then scrape off the loosened paint.

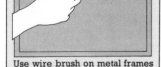
Use wire brush on metal frames

Chipped paint
Remove the old paint, feather-in by rubbing down with a medium glasspaper. Fill the dent with a proprietary cellulose filler and rub smooth. On exterior timber, use a hardwood stopper after applying the primer. Rub down and reprime.

Fill dents with cellulose filler

Crazing
This often occurs when one coat of paint reacts with the one below. Badly affected areas must be stripped back completely and treated as new wood.

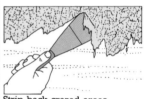
Strip back crazed areas

Sags and Runs
These occur when paint is applied too thickly. The only solution is to strip off the surface and repaint.

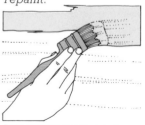
Strip and repaint sags and runs

Flaked surfaces
Scrape back to a firm edge and 'feather' the edges down before repainting.

Feather edges of flaked surface

Pitted, blistered surfaces
Strip back to the bare wood and reprime. Small areas of blistering can be lifted with a knife, the dent primed and filled with stopper. Rub down level with the surrounding surface.

Lift small areas with a knife

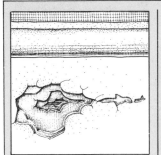
Chipping

Flaking

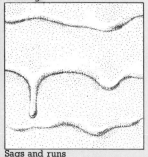
Sags and runs

PAINTING FAULTS

Of the faults shown on this page, most are the result of inadequate preparation, although chipping and flaking may arise through age and hard wear. Sags and runs are directly related to painting technique, but they are easy to avoid.

Pitting/blistering

Crazing

WALL SURFACES

Preparation is the most important part of painting. For most final decorative coats, a level, non-friable, grease-free sub-surface is necessary. Any irregularities will ensure that the finish is less than perfect and also wear less well.

Washing down

On previously painted walls, in good condition, it may only be necessary to wash down well – starting at the bottom of the area to prevent dirty water from running down the wall. Wash down twice thoroughly.

Plaster repairs

Surface cracks

Any cracks in the surface will need cutting out and filling with a proprietary cellulose filler.

Use a cutting knife to enlarge the crack slightly and make a 'V' cut. Clean out any dust and debris and then fill, using the filler to manufacturer's instructions. If the crack is deep it may need filling twice.

Larger damaged areas in the walls may require a plaster repair. Loose plaster, which sounds hollow when tapped, should be hacked back to sound plaster. Remove all dust and debris,

FILLING A CRACK

1. Enlarge the crack and make a V-shaped cut with the scraper.

2. Clean out dust and crumbling plaster with a wire brush.

REPAIRING A HOLE IN PLASTER

1. Cut back until only sound plaster remains; brush out dust.

2. Apply the first layer of filler with a trowel.

Painting walls

damp and then fill with either Keene's cement or a proprietary filler. Apply the filler in one, two, or three layers, cross-hatching each in turn with a trowel tip to provide a key for the next. Once the filler is completely dry rub down level with the surrounding surface.

3. Fill with a standard filler and smooth the surface.

3. Apply subsequent layers, cross-hatching as you go.

USEFUL TIPS

Water based paint finishes
If you are using a decorative emulsion, mix a little of the colour with the filler or plaster. This will make your repair less noticeable when the surface is finally painted.
Oil based paint finishes
If you are using gloss or eggshell-finish paint you will need to apply a coat of primer-sealer, appropriate to the product chosen.

Mix a little of the wall colour with the filler to disguise the repair.

Paint can be applied with a brush, roller, paint pad or spray. Emulsion paint is easier to apply than gloss and should be used on recently plastered areas which are still drying out. On emulsioned walls, a thinned coat of emulsion will provide a satisfactory primer-sealer. The number of paint coats needed depends on the original colour, usually two coats of undercoat and one of top coat will be sufficient. Textured paint finishes should be applied to well-prepared walls in accordance with manufacturer's instructions. Such finishes are useful for hiding minor blemishes and irregularities in surfaces. They should not, however, be used to cover up a defective or unstable sub-surface.

Preparation for paperhanging

Where walls are already papered, old wallcoverings should be completely removed. Use a stripping knife with a 50mm (2in) wide blade and remove as much as possible 'dry'. Next, soak the remaining paper until it starts to blister. Soak workable areas one at a time, starting at the skirting. Use a sponge or a large brush. Stubborn paper may need scoring with the tip of the scraper to allow the water to permeate under the surface and loosen the adhesive. Take care not to dig into the surface. always work horizontally when stripping paper to allow you to keep the stripper at the same angle.

▶
1. Strip as much as possible "dry"
2. Soak remaining paper
3. Score really stubborn areas

VINYL PAPERS

Removing vinyl paper
Vinyl paper is simply removed by making a cut in the corners, peeling back a small section of the surface, and then pulling away the decorative cover, leaving the lining paper beneath, which you can paint over if you choose. You can apply a chemical wallpaper stripper, but for large areas of stubborn wallcovering, it may be worth hiring a steam stripper from a hire shop.

Keying surfaces

When hanging wallcoverings on a previously painted area, key the surface. You can do this by rubbing the surface with pumice stone and water or with a mild abrasive sanding block. Gloss painted surfaces must be sufficiently abraded to remove the gloss, or you will not achieve effective adhesion.

◄ Smoothing down
After any necessary repairs are completed (*see painting*) rub the wall down carefully. You can use either fine glasspaper, garnet paper or a proprietary carborundum block.

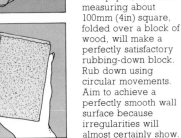
◄ Sanding blocks
Glasspaper, in sheets measuring about 100mm (4in) square, folded over a block of wood, will make a perfectly satisfactory rubbing-down block. Rub down using circular movements. Aim to achieve a perfectly smooth wall surface because irregularities will almost certainly show.

Sizing and lining

Sizing

Before hanging wallcoverings size the wall. This process ensures that the paper adheres evenly. Use the type of size recommended for the type of wallcovering. Fungicidal sizes are available and are suitable for use with all types of wallcoverings, and particularly with vinyls in steamy areas such as kitchens and bathrooms. Always make certain that the wall area is completely dry before hanging the wallcovering because wet size may 'bleed through' the finish surface and blemish it. A dry sized surface should glisten like sugar when looked at against the light.

Lining

Where the walls are sound but not perfectly smooth, or have been painted in a darker colour than the wallcoverings to be used, it is best to line the wall with lining paper, which any good decorating supplier stocks. On really poor surfaces, crossline the walls, lining first vertically and then horizontally. Ensure that the lining paper is completely dry before continuing to work. However, this is not a satisfactory substitute for repairing badly damaged or loose wall plaster.

PAPERHANGING

Pasting procedure

Adhesives

There are two main types of paste, both water soluble. Flour and starch paste mixed with hot or cold water; cellulose water soluble paste, mixed with cold water. Cellulose pastes are generally easier to use and do not stain the surface of the paper. Anaglypta, woodchip and embossed papers are hung with starch flour pastes. Lightweight Anaglyptas, woodchip, vinyl papers and backed fabrics can be hung with cellulose paste. In areas subject to high condensation, such as kitchens and bathrooms, always use a paste containing a fungicide to prevent mould from forming.

Work with the paste table positioned in good light. Keep your tools and materials close at hand. The paste bucket should be easily accessible, but not where it can be stepped on or knocked over. Remember to allow an extra 50mm (2in) for trimming on each length of paper.

2 Charge the pasting brush and start pasting, working outwards from the centre. Spread paste evenly right up to the far edge.

1 Align the cut length with the end and far side of the table. Allow a small overlap so that the paste cannot creep underneath and onto the decorative surface.

3 Position the paper so that it overlaps the front edge of the table and paste this section. Again, work outwards from the centre.

Hanging procedure

4 *Fold the pasted section back on itself and move the folded loop along the table so that it just hangs over the edge. Paste the remainder of the paper as before.*

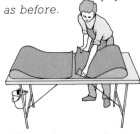

5 *Loop the pasted section back on itself and allow the paste to soak in for a minute or so.*

See page 65

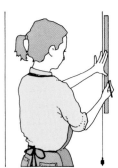

1 *Mark out the room in sections according to the width of the paper, using a plum line or spirit level.*

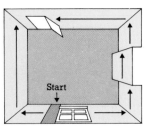

2 *For plain and all-over patterns, start work at the main window area, dividing the room in two halves, and work outwards.*

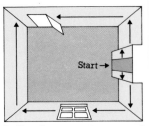

3 *For large patterns and motifs, start work from a focal point, such as a chimney breast, and work outwards.*

4 *Carrying the paper looped over one arm, position the top of the length at the angle between ceiling and wall, lining it up with the marked vertical lines.*

continued overleaf

5 *Allow a trimming overlap top and bottom. Brush outwards from the centre towards the edges. Similarly position and smooth out the bottom loop.*

6 *To trim the paper at top and bottom, mark a cutting line with the back of the shears. Peel the paper back and cut to the score line, then brush back into position.*

7 *Butt-joint the next length of paper; that is, do not overlap the joints but slide the paper into the matching position with the palms of your hands.*

8 *Smooth the edges with a boxwood roller or, for embossed patterns, a felt roller to avoid flattening the design.*

PAPERING PROBLEMS

Papering around doorways

Paste and hang the last full width before the door, leaving 25mm (1in) overlap at the top and at the door edge. At the top of the door frame, make a 150mm (6in) diagonal cut in the paper. Push the paper into the angle between the door and the wall, using the smoothing brush. Score the edges with the shears, trim, and smooth back the paper. On wide door openings, it may be necessary to cut a short length of paper to match in over the centre of the door.

Corners

Place a length of unpasted paper into the corner and mark the line of the angle with the shears. Cut along this line, paste and butt-joint the two pieces into the corner. When hanging paper on projecting corners, allow just 25mm (1in) to overlap the corner. When the pasted paper is in position, trim the overlap to a vertical line. This will correct any discrepancies in the alignment of the wall before hanging the next length.

Fittings

There are two basic methods of papering round switches or similar fittings. The simplest is to remove the switch plate or cover so that the trimming can be done around the hole in the wall or ceiling and will not be visible when the cover is replaced. The other method is to cut the paper into a star shaped hole over the fitting, trim around the

edge of the switch or cover, then smooth the paper up to the edge.

Remove switch plate, if possible.

Stairwells

You have a number of choices for your work sequence. You can start either at the light source, which may be a window or the front door, or, hang the longest length first on the well wall, where it adjoins the headwall, and work in both directions.

As you mark in the vertical lines, allow a 25mm (1in) turn on the headwall (the wall above the staircase) because

the angle may not be true.

Allow the usual trimming overlap at top and bottom. Trim roughly along the stair edge at the cutting angle – this reduces the weight of the paper and stops it pulling as you work. If the paper is very heavy, have someone to support it as you work.

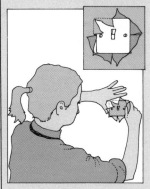

Cut a star shape to fit over the switch or fitting.

MORE PAPERING PROBLEMS

Papering round a window

When using a paper with a bold motif, paper to a plumbed line centrally above the window. Cut the paper long enough to turn under the reveal, adding 50mm (2in) for trimming into the window frame. If the reveal is not true, the pieces turned under may run out of line, in which case allow only a 13mm overlap and cut separate pieces to fill in the gaps. At the edge of each window, cut full length pieces to cover part of the wall and wrap around into the reveal. Work to a plumbed vertical, and allow for the turn and 50mm (2in) for trimming around the frame.

Paste the paper and hang, then crease along the top of the reveal with the back of the shears. Peel away the paper and cut it parallel to the top of the reveal about 50mm (2in) inside the crease mark. Crease and cut the paper in the same way, to fit round the cill. Brush the paper into the reveal. Cut a small piece of paper to fit the remaining unpapered corner.

USEFUL TIP

A string or wire stretched across the paste container will provide a rest for the pasting brush and prevent paste from creeping onto the handle.

Chimney breasts and fireplaces

Whether plain or patterned, the first length should be centred over the fireplace. Allow 25mm (1in) for trimming top and bottom. Hang the outside lengths and make diagonal cuts, as you would for door frames, at the corners of the mantelshelf. Cut round the mantelshelf or moulding, smooth out the paper and trim top and bottom. If a large pattern or motif is not central on the paper, i.e., if the edge of the paper does not run through the centre of the motif, it will be necessary to position the first length slightly to one side in order to centre the motif.

Wallcoverings-minor repairs

Minor repairs and tips
1 If the surface of the paper is wrinkled, it is best to peel back the entire length and reposition it; trying to smooth out large areas of wrinkles will only lead to disaster.
2 To remove small pockets of air or paste, prick the bubble with the point of a sharp knife and carefully smooth out the bump.
3 If gaps appear at the joins, carefully apply a thin coat of PVA adhesive under the edges and smooth down with a roller.
4 You can apply an 'invisible patch' repair on most papers. Cut a matching piece of paper, slightly larger than the damaged area. Soften the cut edges by tearing them. Paste in position and use a seam roller to smooth out, working from the centre to the edges.
5 Patch hessians and vinyls by cutting the new material over the damaged area. Cut through both surfaces at once.

◄Bad wrinkles
The only effective treatment is to peel back the affected area and paste again.

◄Air pockets
The air can be forced out through a small hole made with a knife.

◄Open seams
Usually due to inadequate pasting, or removal of paste during handling. Easily remedied when the paper is in position.

CARRYING PASTED WALLPAPER

Take the paper from the table with the pasted surfaces together. Carry the paper over one arm to the wall, grip the top by the corners and allow to unfold.

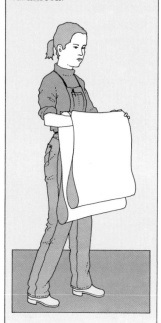

Hanging other wallcoverings

In addition to standard wallcoverings, there are a number of other materials you can use. In the main, they are applied using the same hanging techniques as standard papers, though details may vary according to the product you use.

VINYLS

Once pasted, vinyls can be hung immediately. Make sure that you paste right up to the edge of the paper. When you wish to strip vinyl paper, peel off the vinyl and leave the backing paper which can then be stripped or left as a lining paper.

HESSIANS

These can be backed or unbacked but paper-backed is easier to hang. Use a heavy-duty adhesive, applied with a roller to the wall and to the back of the hessian, but avoid saturating the backing paper. Allow a trimming margin at the top and bottom of the paper and an extra 25mm (1in) overlap on each width.

Mark out the wall in sections, each 25mm (1in) narrower than the hessian. Apply adhesive, and hang each piece using a felt roller to smooth out, with each section's overlapping edges unstuck. Allow the paste to dry. With a sharp handyman's knife held against a metal straight edge, cut through both layers of the overlap; peel away the cut segments and paste the wall beneath. Press back gently along the joint, and firm with a felt seam roller.

FLOCKS

These are highly textured and should be hung with a heavy-duty paste on a lined wall. Use a chamois or rubber-covered roller to smooth down joints.

LINEN

Linen wallcoverings can be unbacked or paper backed. Backed linen is hung in the same way as backed hessian, with heavy-duty adhesive applied to the wall and the backing. Hang unbacked linen with a latex or PVA adhesive.

SILK

Silk should be paper backed because it is easily stained by adhesive bleeding through to the surface. Use a heavy-duty adhesive.

LINCRUSTA

Lincrusta is a heavily moulded wallcovering, available in many colours and in simulated stonework, tiles, wood panelling and fabric effects.

Before hanging this material, size the wall and hang lining paper. Trim the selvedge off the Lincrusta, and cut the pieces to size.

First, soak the back of the Lincrusta with water and allow it to soak in for about 20 minutes, then wipe dry. Apply a starch adhesive to the back of the covering, making sure that you paste right up to the edges.

Offer the piece to the wall, and smooth into position with a rubber roller, ensuring that you work from the centre outwards. Sponge off any adhesive that gets on to the face of the material.

WASHABLES

These are resin-coated papers. Hang with a fungicidal paste, or in non-humid areas, starch or cold-water paste. When stripping these papers, you may need to score the surface to allow water to penetrate the backing paper.

EMBOSSED/TEXTURED

Textured and embossed wallcoverings, including woodgrain paper, are useful for covering minor blemishes in surface areas. Line the wall horizontally before hanging this type of paper. Use a heavy-duty paste. Do not apply heavy pressure to the surface when brushing out or you may flatten the surface. Trim with a sharp knife held against a straight edge.

PATCH REPAIRS TO HESSIAN & VINYL

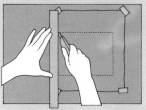

1. Cut a square of new material over the damaged area

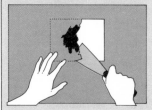

2. Carefully lift out the damaged piece with a stripping knife.

3. Replace with the piece of new material cut at 1.

WALL TILES

Ceramic tiles may be fixed to any clean, reasonably level and stable surface, even to existing tiles, but on rigid partition or stud walls a special flexible adhesive will be needed. When tiling on to an unpainted plaster wall, make sure that any irregularities have been corrected. Paint can be tiled over after washing down and, if it is gloss paint, roughening the surface with sandpaper. All forms of paper wallcovering must be removed. Before tiling new plasterboard, coat the surface with a proprietary sealant or primer. Cork tiles or sheets make an attractive wall finish. Apply these to a clean grease-free, level surface, following the manufacturer's instructions.

Tiling a wall

1 *Room angles are rarely true, so you will need to fix an accurate datum-line to work to. Take one tile, place it at the lowest level of the wall, mark the height of the tile, including any spacer lugs, on the wall and draw a horizontal line.*

2 *Loosely fix a timber batten along this line; check that it is level. Run one tile the length of the batten, checking the batten height from the floor or skirting level.*

3 *Centre the tile on the batten and mark out tile widths to each end. Allow for small gaps between tiles.*

4 *At wall ends, mark the point of the last full tile, and draw a vertical line, using a plumb-bob or a spirit level. The space will be filled in later with cut tiles.*

5 *Spread adhesive on to the wall surface with a notched trowel or applicator.*

6 *Start tiling at the left-hand point and press the tiles into place. Never slide them, because this weakens adhesion. Check that the tiling is even with no tiles proud of the surface.*

7 *Once the main tile area has set, remove the batten and apply adhesive to the backs of the cut tiles and fit into place.*

Grout

This is a compressible white powder which is mixed with water and used to fill the spaces between the tiles. Mix the grout and apply to the face of the tiles using a sponge or squeegee. Wipe off excess grout.

TILING PROCEDURE

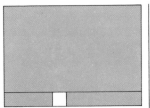
1. Mark datum point

2. Fix batten to marked line

3. Mark tile widths on batten

4. Mark vertical lines at ends

5. Apply adhesive to wall

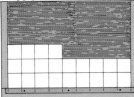
6. Start tiling from left

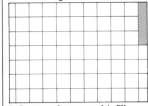
7. Remove batten and infill

8. Grout

CUTTING TILES

Mark the cutting line with a felt-tipped pen. Score along the line to break the tile glaze. Place a matchstick under the tile and press down, exerting pressure firmly on each side of the scored line. The tile should snap evenly; any small projections can be 'nibbled' away using pincers or special tile-cutting tools. To cut shapes in tiles, mark the waste area and 'nibble' it away with sharp pincers. Drill holes using a masonry bit in a power tool, and run at slow speed. For large holes use a radius cutter.

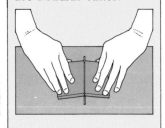

Panelling a wall

Natural wood cladding, as planking or sheet panelling, provides an attractive, warm surface. Once fixed, wood cladding is virtually maintenance free.

Timber panelling is produced in a range of veneers and panel thicknesses, from 4mm ($\frac{3}{16}$in) to 6mm ($\frac{1}{4}$in) and in sheet sizes from 2.4m × 1.22m (8ft × 4ft) to 3.05m × 1.22m (10ft × 4ft).

Timber cladding should be fixed to clean dry plaster. The fixing method used depends on the wall surface. Concrete, brick or insulating blocks are usually battened. Contact adhesive can be used on chipboard, hardboard or plaster surfaces.

Insulation material, such as glass-fibre, quilt or expanded-polystyrene sheet, can be fixed behind the battens.

Do not fix cladding to damp walls. Use rubber or asphalt solution, brushed over the walls or line with 500-gauge polythene sheeting. Also treat the back of the battens with a clear timber preservative.

Timber, panels, or tongued-and-grooved board should be conditioned before fixing by standing in the room where it is to be positioned for about 72 hours.

FIXING BATTENS

Fix vertical battens at 400mm (16in) centres. Horizontal battens, fixed at 300mm (12in) centres., can provide additional fixing. Fix top and bottom battens 25mm (1in) down from the ceiling and 50mm (2in) up from the floor or skirting. Fix vertical battens at each end of the wall, at door openings and round power points; they may need trimming to fit round architraves. Check, with a spirit level, that the battens are level. Where the walls are irregular, pack out cavities behind the battens with slivers of wood. Projections must be smoothed down or the back of the batten shaped to take the projection.
Battens are fixed with masonry nails or screw-fixed into plugged holes using non-rusting screws. Start fixing at a corner of the room.

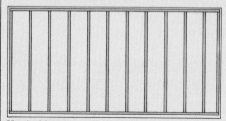

Vertical battens at 40cm (16in) centres ready to receive panelling.

Fixing sheet panelling

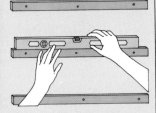

Make sure fitting will be flush with panelling and nail short battens into position.

Check with a spirit level that all battens are square and level.

Use masonry nails or screws to fix the battens to the wall.

Cutting sheet material

Before cutting, score the panel surface with a sharp cutting knife held against a straight edge. A piece of masking tape along the cutting line will ensure a split-free edge. Panels can be cut with a fine toothed panel saw on the face side of the timber. Use a sharp combination blade in a power saw. Cut on the face side of the timber if the saw is hand-held, on the reverse if the saw is bench-mounted.

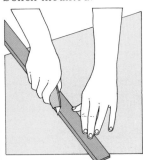

When cutting laminates, cut through the surface and snap against a straight edge.

Scribing

Scribing may be necessary to fit panels to the line of the ceiling or end walls. Place a piece of scrap timber hard to the surface and at right angles to it. Run the timber along the surface with a marking knife or pencil held beneath – scribing the contour on the face of the panel. Cut to this marked line.

Scribing ensures that the last panel will follow the line of the ceiling or end wall.

continued on next page

Fixing sheet panelling
continued from previous page

Fixing with pins
Fix panelling along one length of the room, checking with a spirit level as you work. Dovetail-pin at intervals, through the 'V'-grooves, into the battens. Use 19mm (¾in) or 25mm (1in) panel pins to fix; punch below the surface with a panel punch, then fill the holes using a stopper.

Fixing with glue
Panels can also usually be fixed with contact-adhesive. Apply the adhesive to both the wall and the reverse of the panel. Make sure you position correctly the first time because some brands of adhesive make instant contact. Use masonry pins to fix at high spots.

Cutting holes
To cut a hole in panels, mark out the rectangle with a knife, drill a hole in each corner and cut out with a saw.

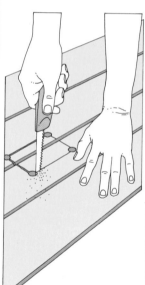

Cutting with pad saw
Use a pad saw to cut out the marked aperture. Finish the edges with a sanding block.

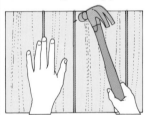

Pin at regular intervals.

Apply glue to battens and panels.

Punch heads below surface and fill.

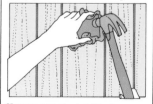

Hammer protected block to spread glue.

Fixing plank panelling

Tongued-and-grooved board or square-edged cladding is usually batten-fixed. Allow a 3 mm ($\frac{1}{8}$in) ventilation at the top and bottom of the cladding. If the ceiling level is uneven, you will need to scribe the planks.

Fix, by secret nailing into the grooves, using 32mm ($1\frac{1}{4}$in) lost-head nails. Pin the first strip through the face of the panel, punch the pin-head below the surface and fill the hole with stopper. Once the first plank is positioned, use a chisel as a lever to cramp each board tightly against the last one fixed. When fixing horizontal panelling, work from the ceiling downwards.

The last two planks cannot be cramped, so these must be 'sprung' into place. Cut them slightly oversize and fit so that they will be slightly bowed – give them a sharp blow with the fist to spring them into place.

Corners

External corners are treated in the following way: cut off the tongue and groove along one length to square the edge. Glue and pin flush to the corner. Repeat this process with the next length to give a neat edge. A wood-stain can be used to match the colour along the edges.

PANEL FIXING TIPS

Score before cutting

◄ **Cutting panelling**
To be sure of a right angled cut, mark out with a knife using a try-square. Cut along the line with a saw in the usual way.

Secret nailing

◄ **Nailing tongue and groove**
Hammer lost head nails into the battens through the grooves of the panelling. Punch the nails below the surface with a pin punch.

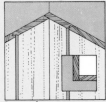

Internal corner

◄ **Fixing at corners**
When using tongue and groove panelling, internal corners can be made by removing the tongue from the last panel and pushing the first panel on the next wall right into the corner – to butt against the one you have trimmed.
External corners can be neatly finished by fixing a strip of edging wood into the angle formed by the end panels.

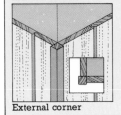

External corner

SUB FLOORS

Renovating solid floors

Types of sub floor

Floors are of two basic types: suspended, consisting of hardwood planks laid over joists, or solid concrete floors. In some older properties floors may be of stone or tiles, sometimes laid directly on to tamped earth.

Most flooring finishes can be applied to either type of surface, but to achieve a good, even, final surface the sub-floor must be correctly prepared. The surface must be clean, level and grease-free.

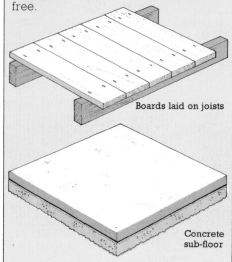

Boards laid on joists

Concrete sub-floor

Self levelling compounds

The most common problem with solid floors is that they become uneven, and disparities in level will mean that any flooring laid over will not wear well or look attractive.

If there are only minor irregularities in the level this can be corrected by using a proprietary self-levelling compound. This is a powder, mixed to a paste with water and floated over the floor. A material, as its name suggests, that will find its own level. Once the self-levelling compound has dried you can lay the final flooring.

Hardboard sub floors

Alternatively, you can use hardboard to create a level sub-surface for a decorative flooring surface. Ensure that the surface is clean and grease-free and use a self-levelling compound to even up the levels, or use a filler. This should consist of a 1:3 cement; a fine sand mix with one part PVA adhesive diluted with three parts water. Trowel the mix and feather off the edges.

If you replace a suspended floor with a screeded floor make sure that there is adequate ventilation to other rooms with suspended floors.

Repairs

Damaged concrete

Large cracks should be filled with a sand/cement/PVA mixture using a trowel. If the floor is badly damaged, screed over the whole area with a steel float. Cover with polythene, or spray with water occasionally, to prevent the screed drying too quickly and cracking.

Laying hardboard to a solid floor

Make sure that the screed and repairs are thoroughly dry. Apply adhesive evenly to the boards – it is not necessary to cover them completely, but ensure that the edges and corners are covered. Follow the sequence shown for laying the boards, then weight them and leave until the adhesive has set.

Use a trowel to fill cracks

Spread screed with a steel float

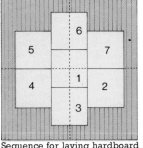

Sequence for laying hardboard

USING HARDBOARD

Hardboard is a satisfactory material to lay as an overfloor before laying cork, linoleum, ceramic tiles and carpeting of various types. Flooring-grade hardboard pinned or glued over the sub-floor will also provide extra sound and thermal insulation. If the sub-floor has been treated with a timber preservative, cover it with a non-porous foil-lining paper to prevent bleeding through to the decorative surface. Where the floor is in damp or humid areas, use an oil-tempered board. Fix the boards at 150mm (6in) centres using 13mm (½in) hardboard nails. Ensure that the joints between the hardboard sheets do not coincide with those in the underlying floorboards.

Renovating floorboards

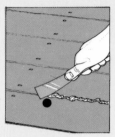

◄Papier-mâché
Small pieces of newspaper, mixed with wallpaper paste or a flour and water paste, will harden sufficiently to make a good filler for small gaps.

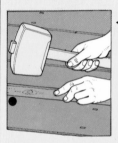

◄Fillets of wood
Small strips, or offcuts of wood can be trimmed to fit the gaps, glued and then tapped into position. When the glue is dry, plane the fillets level with the boards.

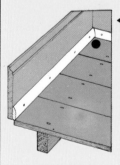

◄Edgings
To fill gaps between floorboards and skirting, you will have to buy quadrant strips and nail, or glue, them into place. Mitre the ends to make neatly fitting corners.

Floorboards should be level, with no projections, such as screws or nails. Where floorboards are uneven they should be lifted and recramped, as necessary, and any badly damaged ones renewed. Where there are small gaps between the board, mix up some papier-mâché and push between the gaps with a filling knife. Papier-mâché consists of postage-stamped sized pieces of newspaper mixed with cold wallpaper paste.

If the floorboards are to remain exposed, mix a little of the final stain with the papier-mâché so that any repair areas blend in with the surrounding boards.

Filled areas should be rubbed smooth. Fillets of wood, glued into place, can be used to fill larger gaps, then planed flush with the surround. Sometimes there are gaps between skirting and flooring, which apart from being unsightly, let in draughts. Small gaps can be filled with a proprietary filler, larger spaces with a wood quadrant strip mitred where edges meet. Major replacement of damaged boards can be undertaken without professional assistance, but it is outside the scope of this book.

Sanding floorboards

To provide a smooth surface for an exposed timber floor, boards should be rubbed down to a perfect finish, and then treated with three coats of coloured or stained polyurethane. These are available in matt or glossy finishes. A floor sander can be hired from a shop. Before using the machine, punch or remove any protruding nail or screw heads. Remove any paint or varnish with a chemical stripper and a metal scraper.

Sanding machines
Drumsanders are used for the large areas of floor; rotary sanders for the edges.

Drum sander

Preparation
Punch all nail heads well below the surface, and make sure that nothing else protrudes.

Second run
Sand, again diagonally, but in the opposite direction. Make sure all sanded strips overlap.

Edges and corners
Using coarse and then fine papers, sand the edges

First run
Sand diagonally to achieve the maximum levelling effect. Keep the machine moving.

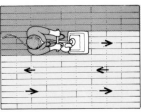

Final run
Use finer papers on the drum to sand along the line of the floor boards.

Decorative finish
Finally, apply sealer, varnish or the flooring paint of your choice.

77

Wood strip flooring

Laying wood strip flooring

Timber flooring must be conditioned, by bringing into the room where it is to be laid, ideally spreading it out and leaving it for at at least 48 hours before starting work.

Remove any doors before starting work. Wood will raise the final level of the floor and doors may need planing to pass smoothly over the new surface.

Where cutting is necessary, use a sharp tenon saw or a power jig saw.

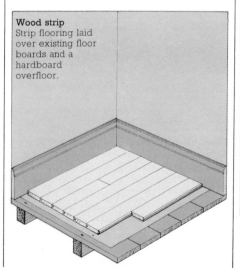

Wood strip
Strip flooring laid over existing floor boards and a hardboard overfloor.

Wood block flooring

Laying wood block flooring

Establish the centre of the floor area – the point from which you start work – then lay the flooring outwards towards the walls. Allow an expansion gap of about 13 mm ($\frac{1}{2}$in) around the wall edge. This is best accommodated beneath the skirting, but you can use a cork expansion strip or a cover strip which makes a neat join between floor and skirting board. Use PVA adhesive on cut edges to prevent blocks splitting apart.

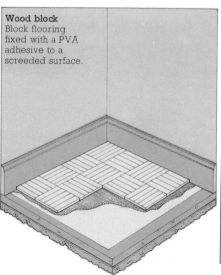

Wood block
Block flooring fixed with a PVA adhesive to a screeded surface.

TYPES OF WOOD FLOORING

Wood block
Wood blocks are available in a range of sizes and thicknesses. The wood may be solid blocks or wood veneer bonded to a thinner, plywood block. These may come presealed or supplied ready for final smoothing down and sealing.

End-grain block
End-grain block is a very hard-wearing flooring surface. Lay with the end grain exposed.

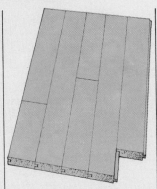

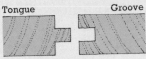

Tongue   Groove

Strip-wood flooring
This consists of tongued-and-grooved looselaid interlocking panels. Some stripwood flooring materials are supplied with a cork or polythene backing-sheet, laid before the panels are fixed. This is important when laying on to a concrete sub-floor.

Parquet and mosaics
Parquet and mosaic wood flooring may consist of panels of several tiles which are stuck down in one operation. Mosaics are generally in patterns such as basket-weave or herring-bone. Panels are generally felt-backed or paper-backed. Paper-backed panels are laid with the paper uppermost, which is later removed by sanding after the panels are laid. Felt-backed panels are laid with the felt downwards.

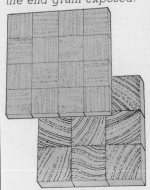

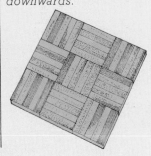

Laying vinyl or cork

Vinyl or cork floor tiles should be laid on a level, clean and dry surface using the adhesive recommended by the manufacturer.

Tools

You will need a pencil, ruler, a block of wood about 150mm (6in) long, a handyman's knife, a piece of chalk, a length of string, adhesive and a notched adhesive spreader. However some tiles are adhesive-backed and once the floor is set out, the adhesive can be activated by dipping the tiles in hot water or, in some cases by peeling off a backing paper. Many flooring materials benefit by being brought into the room where they will be laid 48 hours before starting work, to condition the tiles. This is very important if you are using cork.

Cutting tiles ▶
Score along a marked line with a sharp knife and the tiles will then snap cleanly. Cork and linoleum tiles should be cut on the face side.

SETTING OUT

Divide the room exactly in half and snap a chalked string line across the length and breadth of the floor to provide a cruciform. The point where the lines meet provides the datum point from which tiling starts. If this is not central and square the tiling will not be square.

Place the tiles loosely along the lines, working towards the walls, but do not fix them at this stage. This allows you to establish whether you should displace the chalk cruciform reference to allow an even tiling arrangement and avoid odd cuts at room edges.

Begin tiling from where the chalk lines intersect. Apply adhesive (if appropriate) to an area of about 1sq m (1sq yd). Apply thinly with a notched spreader and lay the first tile at the intersection working outwards. Apply the adhesive to the under edges of tiles on the chalk line, so preventing tiles from lifting along the edges. Press evenly around the edges of each tile, then in the middle.

Use a rubber roller to smooth down each section of tiles as they are laid. Once the main tiles have been laid you will have to cut others to fill in the gaps between the last full tile and the walls.

Laying edge tiles

Measuring for cutting

If the gap between the last full tile and the wall is even along the edge of the wall, place the tile to be cut over the corresponding tiles in the last complete row. Take a spare tile and place it over the tile to be cut and mark the amount of overlap on the bottom of the tile. Cut this off.

Where the gap between the wall and the last complete line of full tiles is not even, use a spare tile as a marker to show the distance variations. Put the tile to be trimmed on the final complete tile; join the two marks with a ruler line, and cut the tile along the ruled line to fit.

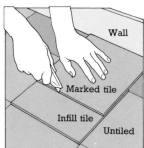

Use a tile as a guide

Wall

Marked tile

Infill tile

Untiled

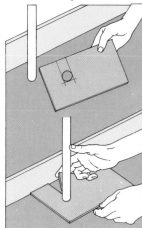

Cutting around an obstacle
Mark the position of the obstacle on the tile, cut a slit from the edge and a hole for the obstacle, then ease the tile into position.

CUTTING SHAPES

When laying floor tiles it will be necessary to cut round profiles such as door frames or corners. You can use a spare tile for this. Position the tile to be cut on top of the corresponding tile in the last row before the corner or frame. Hold the spare tile vertically, parallel with the run of the floor and mark off the shape of the corner. When these points are joined, the profile of the corner is reproduced on the tile. Cut the tile and fit it into position.

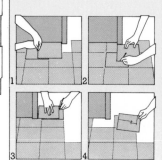

Laying sheet material

FITTING SHEET FLOORING

You will need a ruler, a pencil, a lino cutting tool, handyman's knife or scissors, a piece of chalk, a length of string, a piece of timber 150mm (6in) long for scribing and, possibly, a roll of self-adhesive tape.

Sheet flooring is conditioned by bringing into the room before it is laid for about 48 hours – this makes it more pliable and easier to manage when you start work. Always lay flooring of the same width in one area.

Where the product chosen has a matched edge pattern, stick the joins with an adhesive tape, but do not fix at the edges of the room. Work with the material so that the pattern matches both along the length and across the width of the room. Position the first length along the longest wall, place the second length beside it.

The wall contours of a room are rarely true, so you will have to scribe flooring to fit. Position the first strip of flooring along the edge of the longest wall in the room, leaving a 50mm (2in) overlap at each end of the length.

Draw a line on the skirting board and on the flooring 300mm (12in) from the end wall. Pull the flooring back slowly until the distance between the mark on the skirting and that on the flooring is 150mm (6in) the length of the timber block.

Leave the flooring in this position while you use the block to scribe the contours of the wall onto the flooring. Cut along the marked line.

The 50mm (2in) overlap is now eliminated and the flooring will fit perfectly when pushed back into the corner.

Loose flooring ▶
Loose-laid flooring should be stuck along the joins with a self-adhesive tape.

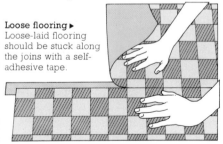

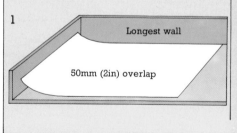

1

Longest wall

50mm (2in) overlap

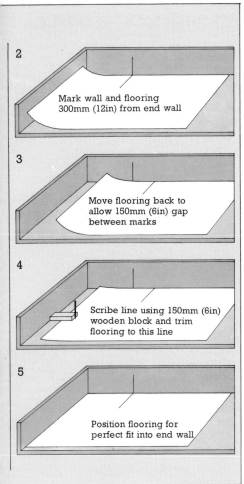

2

Mark wall and flooring 300mm (12in) from end wall

3

Move flooring back to allow 150mm (6in) gap between marks

4

Scribe line using 150mm (6in) wooden block and trim flooring to this line

5

Position flooring for perfect fit into end wall

Fitting sheet material around doorways and projections

When laid, the flooring should be trimmed so that it finishes exactly halfway under the door in a closed position. Fitting in round doorways and projections, such as chimney breasts, is simple if you follow the sequence shown. You can use a piece of card or a proprietary template former to mark the profile on the flooring.

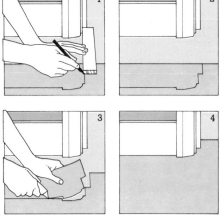

Cutting to fit
Using a wood block, or a template, mark the shape of the projection on the flooring and cut it out with a sharp knife.

Laying ceramic tiles

You can tile on to screed or timber floors. They must be clean and grease-free. If the tiles are particularly heavy, the floor may need bracing. Suspended timber floors can be strengthened with a sheet plywood floor, screw-fixed, at 300mm (12in) centres. When tiling bathrooms or shower areas, lay a damp-proof membrane and use waterproof adhesive and grouting. You can use proprietary adhesives to fix tiles to timber floors. The following is a typical method of laying ceramic floor tiles, using a bonding agent, adhesive and grout.

Tools

For tiling, you will need the following tools: a notched spreader, pincers, tile-cutter, sponge, squeegee. You will also need a bonding agent, adhesive and grout.

Laying tiles ▶
Spread the adhesive with a notched spreader. Using card as spacer lugs, press tiles into place.

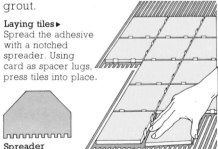

Spreader

SETTING OUT

Divide the floor into four sections. First, snap a chalked string line from the centre of the doorway to the farthest wall. Next, snap a second line, at right angles to the first, across the width of the room.

Place a line of tiles, loose laid, along each marked line, adjusting as necessary, to leave equal spacing for cut tiles at the wall edges (ideally half a tile). Where this is not possible, remove one tile and adjust the remaining tiles to give a longer space at each end. Some tiles have spacer lugs which give a 3 mm ($\frac{1}{8}$in) gap. On non-lugged tiles – use pieces of stiff card to keep a 3mm ($\frac{1}{8}$in) grouting gap.

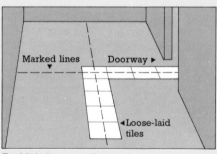

Marked lines ▾   Doorway ▶

◀ Loose-laid tiles

Establish the centre lines and loose lay a row of tiles from wall to wall. Adjust to leave half tiles spaces at walls.

APPLYING THE TILES

Brush a bonding agent generously over the entire floor area and allow to become touch dry. Mix the powder adhesive with water until it is a creamy consistency. Allow this to stand and thicken for about 20 minutes. Stir immediately before use, and spread. Use a notched spreader to rib the adhesive. This aids adhesion. Cover an area of 1 sq m (1 sq yd) at a time. Place each tile firmly into place, using a slight twisting action to counteract any skin forming on the adhesive and ensure good adhesion. Clear off any adhesive on the tile face.

Lay the main field tiles first, working towards the walls. Check for tile creep. At the edges, cut the tiles to fit. If the surface has a high glaze, score the back of the tile. 'Butter' the back of individual cut tiles before positioning. Any rough edges can be nibbled away with pincers. Do not force cut tiles into place.

Leave to set for 24 hours to allow the adhesive to bond. Mix the flooring grout to a thick paste, tip out on to the tiled area and work firmly into the joints with a squeegee or the smooth back of a spreader. Allow the grout to harden for at least an hour before cleaning.

Laying quarry tiles

You will need the following tools: a small chisel, a hammer, a pair of pincers, an abrasive carborundum stone, or a carborundum disc in a power drill.

Quarry tiles are very dense and hard and may be difficult to cut. Mark the cutting line along the tile and use a hammer and chisel to make indentations on the surface.

Place a brick on the ground and, gripping the tile firmly in both hands, strike it against the edge, along the marked line.

You can remove rough edges with pincers. Curved edges should be marked and indented in the same way and projections removed with pincers or smoothed with a carborundum stone.

Alternatively, you can use a glass-fibre carborundum disc in a circular power saw to cut quarries. Wear goggles for safety.

Lay on a prepared sub-floor (see *preparation*), in a 1:3 (mortar–sand) mortar bed. Before laying, soak the tiles and, once laid, make sure that they are level before grouting with an equal part sand/cement grout. Allow a few days for the floor to set.

Decorating ceilings

Ceilings preparation

All ceilings must be prepared carefully before decorating. Cracks must be cut back, filled with a proprietary filler and sanded down when dry. Adequate safe access, across the width of the room, is essential when working. (See *Safety*).

◄ **Papering ceilings**
Support the folded portions of the pasted paper with a block of wood or a roll of paper. Holding the paper to the ceiling, brush towards the wall. Brush the centre of the strip first, then the edges.

◄ **Painting ceilings**
Ceilings should be painted in strips about 60cm (2ft) wide. If you are unable to use ladders or trestles, you could try the extended roller shown here. This enables you to paint from the floor, but you will not have so much control.

PAPERING & LINING CEILINGS

Estimating materials

You will need to find the area of the ceiling by multiplying length by width and buying the number of rolls required for this area. Paper manufacturers will indicate the coverage of their product.

Setting out

Start work at the main window area and work away from it. This will ensure that the joins are in shadow and less visible. Work to a right angled guide line for the first length. This can be marked using a pencil and a chalked line. Marking the chalked line is a two-handed job. Measure the width of the paper from the corner of the room and mark lightly with a pencil. Mark out the same distance on the other side of the room and 'twang' the chalked line between these points. This gives the working guide line. Measure and cut the paper, allowing a 50mm (2in) overlap, for trimming, at each end. At this stage, cut all the lengths required to finish the area.

Pasting

Paste the paper as for wallcoverings but fold in concertina fashion. Paste the first length, fold one end over in a 300mm (12in) pleat, next fold over a 600mm (24in) pleat and then turn back the first 300mm (12in) pleat. Repeat this fold sequence until you reach the last 600mm (24in). Turn this back 300mm (12in) to join the concertina folds.

Support the folded paper on a short timber batten, or a roll of paper, as you lift it to the ceiling.

Papering the ceiling

With the chalked guide line on your left, position the paper. Unroll the first fold, holding the concertina close to the ceiling and brushing it out, from the middle to the sides, into its final position. Move along the trestle, unfolding and brushing out the paper as you go.

A useful aid to support the concertina as you work, is a 'dead man's hand'. This is a spring-loaded pole with a wooden platform on top which supports the paper. You can make a simple aid of this sort from a long timber batten with a cross-piece.

At the angle between the walls and ceiling, press the paper in firmly and score with the back of the shears along this line. Peel the paper back carefully and trim, leaving a 6mm ($\frac{1}{4}$in) overlap which you then press back into position on the wall.

Papering round light fittings

Mark out each length as you work. When you reach a light fitting, cut the paper in a star-shape so that it can be pushed over the fitting and trimmed.

Alternatively: locate the centre of the fitting, make two cuts, one in the direction you are applying the paper, the other at right angles to it, press back the flaps, score and trim, then press the paper back into position.

Papering the frieze

The frieze is usually papered to match the ceiling paper. Measure the depth of the frieze, adding 50mm (2in). Cut the same number of frieze pieces as the number of lengths across the room. Paste and fold the pieces lining up each section at the right-hand corner with the ceiling paper. Brush out the paper and trim off the excess.

Ceiling treatments

Painting ceilings

Before painting make sure the ceiling area is completely clean and grease-free. If there are damaged or unstable areas repair as necessary (see *plaster repairs*). On previously distempered ceilings remove all traces of this material. It is a time consuming job, but if any distemper is left the new surface will not adhere. Use a large brush or a roller to apply paint.

Polystyrene ceilings

Sheet polystyrene can be used for ceiling areas. This is fixed in the same way as ceiling paper, using a suitable adhesive – usually a polystyrene cement. Spread the adhesive evenly across the material. Do not spot fix because this adds to fire hazard.

Paint polystyrene tiles with a water-based paint, such as emulsion, and never use gloss paint which renders them highly flammable.

Tiling ceilings

Ceiling tiles of cork, wood fibre or polystyrene are attractive ceiling finishes. The method used for setting out is exactly the same as that used for floor tiles. Find the centre each side of the ceiling and position the chalk line from the marked points. 'Twang' the chalk line to divide the ceiling into four sections. Where the lines intersect is the centre point of the ceiling.

Tiling starts at the centre unless you are using flanged edged tiles, in which case you start at one corner. As it is unlikely that the ceiling area will accommodate an exact number of full tiles, adjust the centre point to ensure that the cut tiles at the ceiling edges are of equal size.

Position four tiles at the centre point, one into each right-angle. If these centre tiles are aligned correctly all the rest of the tiles will line up accurately.

Work from the centre of the room outwards. Once the tiles in the main area are fixed, cut any part tiles you may need and fix them into position.

Flanged tiles

Position flanged tiles with the flange outwards, and start tiling at one corner of the ceiling. Keep an even 150mm (6in) border round the room.

Check the distance across the ceiling, at several points. If these measurements vary, add the odd millimetres to each border. Mark the border space with a chalked line along both short and long lengths of the ceiling.

Scribe the first tile and cut on the scribed line. The grooved edge should be on the waste side of the tile. Position the tile between the chalk-marked line and the wall.

Panelled ceilings

Timber cladding is available in interlocking panels. You will need to fix a softwood batten framework to the ceiling to receive the panels. Fix battens to ceiling joists. You may need to adjust the panel sizes so that the joins between them will match the line of the patterns.

If you have to cut the panels, mitre the edges to give a neat 'V' joint. Fix with 25mm (1in) panel pins, nailing at an angle, every 300mm (12in) and every 150mm (6in) at the edges. This is normally a two-man job but you can use a dead-man's hand to support the panel while fixing.

Alternatively, you can use planks for cladding. They may consist of PVC or timber. PVC cladding may be fixed with losthead nails, through the grooved edges into battens, or directly into the joists.

Timber planking may be fixed diag-onally across a ceiling area, along the length or across the width, to a batten framework. Planking is easier to fix than timber panels.

All timber for cladding should be conditioned before fixing. Ideally it should be stood for up to seven days in the room where it is to be fixed.

Hardboard and insulating board can also be ceiling fixed, generally to a batten framework.

Illuminated ceilings

An effective and decorative way of lowering a ceiling, or disguising one that is unattractive, is to install an illuminated ceiling.

Provision must be made for effective lighting, usually fluorescent tube lights, because the PVC panels that make up the false ceiling absorb up to 50 per cent of the light emitted.

Before fixing an illuminated ceiling clean the original area thoroughly. You can line with aluminium foil or high-gloss white paint – which will help to deflect light downwards. If you use aluminium foil, fix with a fungicidal paste. The area above the panels, especially in humid areas such as kitchens, can be a breeding ground for mould.

Glossary of terms

Architrave
The fixed framework of a door or window. The word is most often used to refer to the mouldings which usually form part of the frame.

Casement
A window arrangement usually consisting of some fixed and some hinged lights. The term is also applied to projecting windows involving side lights – familiar in older houses.

Charging
The expression used for loading a brush with paint.

Cruciform
The arrangement of door panels in which the central (non-recessed) areas form the shape of a cross.

Filling
The name given to the bristles of a brush.

Frieze
The area between picture rail and ceiling, or between architrave moulding and cornice.

Laying off
A technique used when painting which involves lifting the brush towards the edge of the painted area – thus avoiding a 'lip' or ridge of paint.

Picture rail
A strip of moulding fixed horizontally to a wall, usually about 7ft 6in (2.3m) from the floor. Not found in modern houses, it was originally intended, as the name suggests, as a device from which to hang pictures.

Primer
The first coat of varnish, paint or sealer, applied to provide a suitable surface for subsequent coats.

Rails (*doors*)
The areas of the door which run between and around the panels. In other words, the parts of a door which are not recessed. On a cruciform door each rail will consist of one piece of wood.

Reveal
The recessed area of wall formed by windows and, sometimes, doorways.

Sash
The weighted cords used in the older style of vertically opening window.

Screed
A layer of (usually) concrete used to level the surface of a floor.

Scribing
Making a line with a sharp edge or point.

Soffits
The wooden boards which are apparent on some houses just below the eaves.

Conversion tables

How to use the charts
The centre column refers to the units of measurement and may be either imperial or metric. To convert one litre to gallons: find I in the centre column and look for the answer. To convert gallons to litres: start in the centre and look to the left hand column.

1000 millilitres = 1 litre
10 millimetres = 1 centimetre
100 centimetres = 1 metre
100 grams = 1 kilogram
1000 kilograms = 1 tonne

● NB All figures rounded up or down to the nearest convenient figure.

LIQUIDS

LITRES (l)	LITRES OR GALLONS	GALLONS (gals)
4.55	1	0.20
9.10	2	0.45
13.65	3	0.65
18.20	4	0.09
22.75	5	1.10
27.30	6	1.30
31.80	7	1.55
36.40	8	1.75
40.90	9	2.00
45.45	10	2.20
90.90	20	4.40
136.00	30	6.60
182.00	40	8.80
227.00	50	11.00

WEIGHT

KILOGRAMS (Kg)	KILOGRAMS or POUNDS	POUNDS (lbs)
0.45	1	2.20
0.90	2	4.40
1.35	3	6.60
1.80	4	8.80
2.30	5	11.00
2.70	6	13.25
3.20	7	15.45
3.65	8	17.65
4.10	9	19.85
4.55	10	22.05
10.00	20	44.10
13.60	30	66.15
18.15	40	88.20
22.70	50	110.20

LINEAR

MILLIMETRES (mm)	MILLIMETRES or INCHES	INCHES (ins)
25	1	0.40
50	2	0.80
75	3	1.20
100	4	1.60
125	5	2.00
150	6	2.40
175	7	2.80
200	8	3.20
230	9	3.50
250	10	3.90
600	20	7.90
760	30	11.80

Primer and paint use guide

INTERIOR WORK

SURFACE	PRIMERS & PREPARATION	PAINT	OTHER POINTS
Woodwork & man-made boards	One coat of leadless primer applied after knotting	Emulsion paint; apply two coats	Thin with water
	Knot and prime (leadless); apply at least one undercoat	Oil paint; one or two coats	Thin with white spirit; a durable easy-clean impervious finish
	On new-stripped wood, use knotting and primer	Plastic paints; one or two-coat finish	Non-drip (thixotropic) or gel; do not thin or stir unless using a roller
	Follow the maker's instructions	Polyurethane; one or two-coat finish	Thin initially with 20 per cent white spirit; hard, high-quality finish
Ceilings, walls and wall boards	Use thinned coat as sealer on absorbent surfaces	Water paint (distemper); two coats	Thin with water; not washable or very durable
	As above	Oil-bound distemper; two-coat finish	More durable than above
	Ensure surface is free from dust	Emulsion paints; two-coat finish	Thin with water; washable
Ceilings, walls and wall boards	As above; apply to dry surface only	Oil paint; two-coat finish	Thin with turpentine or white spirit; washable; do not use on new plaster
	Leadless primer; may be thinned to seal dusty or absorbent surfaces	Plastic paints; one or two-coat finish	As for oil paint
Ferrous metals (e.g. iron)	Clean surface and prime with metallic primer	Oil paint; two-coat finish	Thin with turpentine or white spirit
Non-ferrous metals (e.g. copper, brass)	Clean with wire wool and white spirit; prime with metal primer	Oil paint; two-coat finish	Thin with turpentine or white spirit

Primer and paint use guide

EXTERIOR WORK

SURFACE	PRIMERS & PREPARATION	PAINT	OTHER POINTS
Woodwork	Knot and prime; use two under-coats	Oil paint; three-coat finish	Paint on dry surface in warm, dry weather
	Ensure surface is grease-free; timber may be stained before varnishing	Oleoresin or resin varnish; synthetic varnish	As above
Walls	Scrub surface to remove organic growth and loose particles	Cement paints; two-coat finish	Surface may craze
	As above	Latex-based paints; one or two-coats	A flexible finish
	As above	External-quality emulsion; two-coats	Not as durable as a cement- or latex-based paint
	Scrub surface free of loose particles; use primer on dry surface	Oil paint; two or three-coat finish	Use over rendered surfaces only
Ferrous metals (e.g. iron)	Clean surfaces; use with metal primer	Oil paint; three-coat finish	Apply only in warm, dry weather
Asbestos	Remove organic growth and loose particles	Chlorinated rubber or bitumen-based	Only use oil-based paints if recommended

Index

Figures in italics
refer to illustrations

Acknowledgments

The 'How To' Book of
Home Decorating was
created by Simon Jennings
and Company Limited.
We are grateful to the
following individuals and
organisations for their
assistance in the making
of this book:

Arthur Baker: *line illustrations*
Brian Craiker: *line illustrations*
The Dover Archive: *engravings and embellishments*
FADS Homecare Centres: *decorating tools and equipment*

Photographs:
John Couzins: cover, title page and pages **14–15**, **22–23**
Dunlop: page **19** *br*
Gerflex Ltd.,: page **19** *t*
Harrison Drapes: page **26** *tl*
ICI Paints Division: pages **11** *t*; **31** *br*
Interlubke: page **26** *bl*
Nelson King Associates: page **78** *br*
Langley London Ltd.: **10** *tl*; **31** *tl*
Luxaflex Fineblinds: page **27** *t*
Bill Maclaughlin: pages **10** *bl*; **19** *bl*; **30** *tl*; and *bl*;
31 *tr*
Sonia Roberts: page **27** *b*
Sanderson Triad: pages **11** *bl*; **27** *b*
Wicanders (GB) Ltd.; page **18** *l*
2B Building Plastics: page **10** *br*

abbreviations: *t* top; *b* bottom; *c* centre; *tl* top left; *tr* top right;
bl bottom left; *br* bottom right; *r* right

Typesetting by Servis Filmsetting Ltd., Manchester
Headline setting by Facet Photosetting, London

Special thanks to Norman Ruffell and
the staff of Swaingrove Ltd., Bury St. Edmunds,
Suffolk, for the lithographic reproduction.

'HOW TO'